MW01600902

Authentic Health Care Marketing

BUILD TRUST, ENGAGE PATIENTS, AND SUCCEED IN THE POST-TRUTH ERA

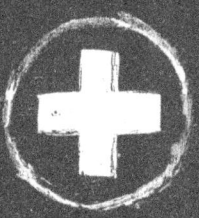

BRANDON EDWARDS

WITH SHANNON McINTYRE HOOPER

AUTHENTIC HEALTHCARE MARKETING

BUILD TRUST, ENGAGE PATIENTS, AND SUCCEED IN THE POST-TRUTH ERA

BRANDON EDWARDS

WITH SHANNON McINTYRE HOOPER

Designed by Dino Marino Design, www.dinomarinodesign.com

E-book ISBN: 979-8-9928740-1-3
Paperback ISBN: 979-8-9928740-0-6
Hardcover ISBN: 979-8-9928740-2-0

SPECIAL INVITATION

Scan the QR code below to get the free resource we've created detailing big-picture takeaways to help you apply what you've learned in *Authentic Healthcare Marketing*.

To the 4,300,000 nurses and 989,320 physicians
around the country who dedicate their lives
to the health of others.
You became known as heroes during the COVID era
because that's exactly what you are.

CONTENTS

INTRODUCTION

My mother died of colon cancer at sixty-eight years old. She hadn't been to a doctor in nearly thirty years.

She and my father were uninsured by choice for more than two decades. My mother never had a colonoscopy or a mammogram. She refused to have those preventative procedures partly because she bought into a radical belief that exists in our post-truth era.

She came to believe that if she went to doctors, they would put her on all kinds of medicine that would produce side effects that made her sick. In effect, she believed healthcare made you sick. Therefore, she refused to go.

As a result, her life was cut short. She and my father had been married for forty-eight years and had known each other since grade school.

They certainly could have purchased health insurance, especially after the passage of the Affordable Care Act. They even had traditional Medicare later in life, yet they still didn't go to doctors.

Because my mom believed the healthcare system was bad for her, she thought having a colonoscopy would "stir things up" and cause you to have cancer. Furthermore, after her diagnosis, she and my father came to believe in unproven therapies outside of more traditional cancer care.

None of those helped, but they certainly helped the people who sold them for thousands of dollars.

They even avoided going to what is arguably one of the best colorectal cancer centers in the world, at Stanford, a three-hour drive away. Instead, they went to their local community hospital because the people there said all cancer care was basically on a formula, and they followed the same one as "those big academic medical centers." This might have been true with specific cancers or specific patients; however, it was not true for my mother and her health situation.

She was convinced there was no difference in the quality of care from one hospital to another. Sadly, she was wrong in this case, and she passed away eleven months later.

When it comes to your healthcare choices, every decision matters, both big and small ones.

MARKETING IS ABOUT CONNECTION

This story—obviously a very personal one to me—has in many ways informed my view on marketing. In what I call our "post-truth era" (a term I'll unpack a little later), marketing isn't just about how you feel, whether you like the brand, or if the graphics are pretty. Healthcare marketing is all about connecting people to the care they need so they can live better lives.

HEALTHCARE MARKETING IS ALL ABOUT CONNECTING PEOPLE TO THE CARE THEY NEED SO THEY CAN LIVE BETTER LIVES.

As marketing professionals, we fill an incredibly important gap for people. Our goal is to help them understand the healthcare system and learn how to choose the doctors and hospitals that are best for them. You may believe that this should be done by health insurance payors or the government, but it falls to hospitals and health systems and other healthcare providers to do it themselves.

Through the experience of seeing my mother's worldview directly affect her opinions about healthcare (and how it shortened her life), I learned to have more empathy for people who see the world differently from me. I'm not sure I qualify as an empath in all areas, but good marketers must show compassion for the people they reach and meet them where they are. That's the only way our work can be effective.

As was the case with my mother, there are very real consequences to believing certain things about healthcare.

Authentic Healthcare Marketing isn't just another marketing or business book. I'm not here to dispassionately dissect a topic like an academic writing a dissertation. I truly care about marketing in the healthcare space and the way it helps people.

This isn't just a job for me. It's my passion and my purpose. I've seen time and again how someone's worldview has a real-world impact on their life—and sometimes, the end of their life.

THE QUESTION I'M TRYING TO ANSWER

The key assumption driving this book is that our approach to healthcare marketing needs to be fundamentally different from what it was ten or even five years ago. The term "post-truth era" has been in the public discourse for decades, yet we now undeniably live in a post-truth era where our cultural institutions and traditional sources of truth and authority have eroded.

How serious is this? One example is the twenty-fifth anniversary edition of the Edelman Trust Barometer, which revealed a profound shift to acceptance of aggressive action, with political polarization and deepening fears giving rise to a widespread sense of grievance.

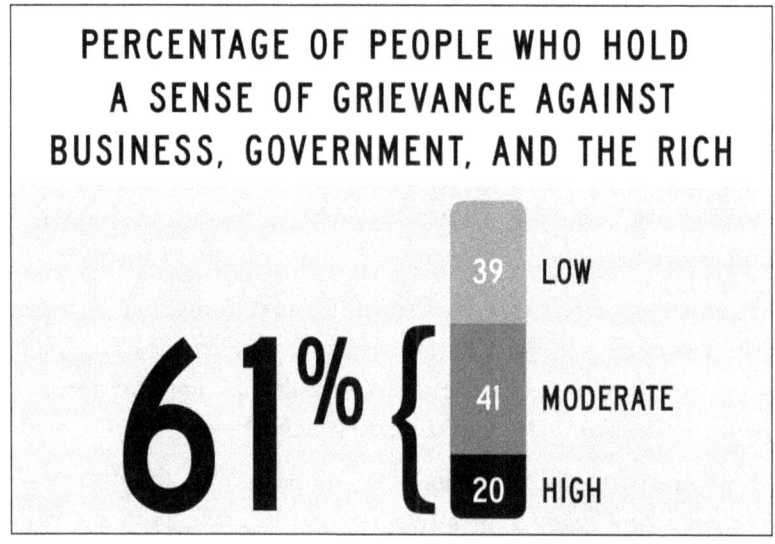

PERCENTAGE OF PEOPLE WHO HOLD A SENSE OF GRIEVANCE AGAINST BUSINESS, GOVERNMENT, AND THE RICH

61% {
39 LOW
41 MODERATE
20 HIGH

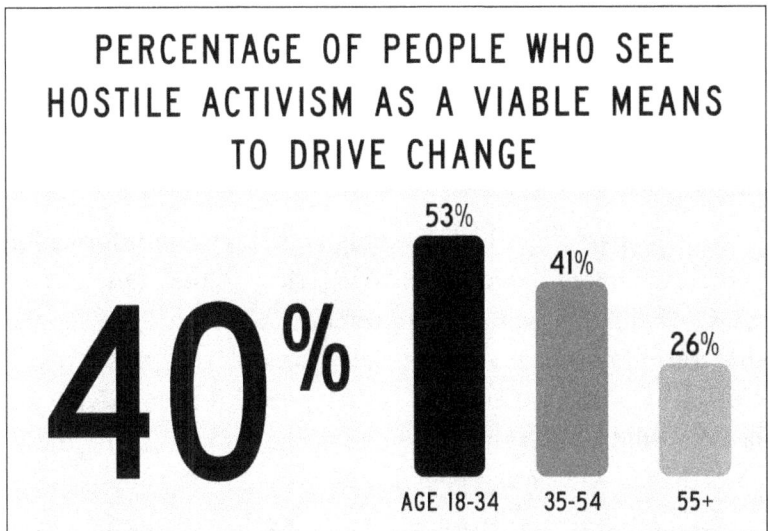

Most people in this cohort hold grievances against government, business, and the rich; 61 percent globally have a moderate or high sense of grievance, which is defined as a belief that government and business make their lives harder and serve narrow interests, and wealthy people benefit unfairly from the system. While not part of the study, many patients perceive doctors and healthcare executives, and thus the healthcare system, to be part of the wealthy or using the government as a source of illegitimate gain.

Hostile activism is seen as a legitimate tool to drive change. For example, 40 percent of Edelman respondents said they would approve of one or more of the following forms of hostile activism: attacking people online, intentionally spreading disinformation, threatening or committing violence, and/or damaging public or private property. This sentiment is most prevalent among respondents ages eighteen to thirty-four (53 percent of that group approve of at least one form).[1]

---

1   Edelman. "2025 Edelman Trust Barometer." Edelman Trust Institute, January 2025, https://www.edelman.com/trust/2025/trust-barometer

In practice, this post-truth era means that people look to all kinds of influencers and nontraditional media sources for their information now. In this atmosphere it is no surprise that there is a decline in trust in our institutions in general and healthcare in particular.

The January 2025 KFF Tracking Poll on Health Information and Trust showed that confidence in "science," the FDA, and the CDC is falling.[2] Advisory Board research in January 2025 showed that trust in doctors is at its lowest level in over twenty-five years.[3] Unlock's Consumer Compass 2024 reported that consumers see hospitals and health systems as more to blame for rising healthcare costs than insurance companies.

In an industry that is dealing with life and death on a daily basis, trust is fundamental. Society needs to be able to trust its healthcare system, and today we don't.

What does this mean to you as a healthcare marketer? In some cases, the Edelman Trust Barometer study shows why some patients or their families feel it is righteous to show up to the hospital with a gun, ready to punish those who they feel may not have treated their family well or as they expected (this could be treatments, attitudes, or attention).

In this cultural context, how does a healthcare company, health system, or physician practice use authentic marketing to reach consumers and patients, connect with them, and help them make the right choices for themselves? How do we do that when the information and factors that drive patients' choices may not be what you would endorse or support?

---

2 KFF, "KFF Tracking Poll on Health Information and Trust: January 2025," last modified January 28, 2025, https://www.kff.org/health-information-and-trust/poll-finding/kff-tracking-poll-on-health-information-and-trust-january-2025/

3 Advisory Board, "See how American trust in healthcare is falling, in 5 charts," Advisory Board Daily Briefing, January 30, 2025, https://www.advisory.com/daily-briefing/2025/01/30/health-information-trust-poll

This is why I believe in a concept that I call Authentic Healthcare Marketing, which at its simplest is defined as follows:

Authentic Healthcare Marketing is the process of communicating a healthcare brand's key messaging that is rooted in your mission, values, and strategy and helps the right audience connect with, believe in, and trust your message.

That's the main topic this book is designed to discuss. In doing so, I hope that you'll come away with three things:

First, I will explain the current cultural context (the post-truth era) and why it is so challenging for healthcare organizations to design and execute effective, authentic marketing. We'll also dive into what "authentic" marketing means.

Second, I will walk you through five "mile markers" that healthcare companies can use to leverage more authentic marketing.

And third, I want to cast a vision for a more hopeful future, where healthcare companies can connect with consumers, their patients, clients, and customers in a way that serves them well—even when they aren't getting their information from traditional sources or sometimes even the most accurate sources.

My guess is that you have come to this book looking for healthcare marketing solutions that work in the current climate. As a marketer, you feel busy and often overwhelmed. I want to give you strategic, practical solutions for your marketing that actually work.

In the process, I want to challenge you to think differently about your organization's brand and how you market your healthcare services.

WHY I WROTE THIS BOOK

The main audience I am writing this book for is marketers inside healthcare provider organizations, including CMOs and their staff in hospitals, health systems, physician groups, and digital health companies. These are the people devoting their lives to explaining this complicated and emotionally laden healthcare system we are all forced to navigate.

If you are in the business of communicating with a group of people to help them understand what you do when they need care, you've come to the right place.

However, I also had a second group in mind when writing this book: the C-suite and boards inside those organizations, including CEOs, CFOs, CSOs, board members, and others who have a vested interest in your organization's marketing but don't have day-to-day responsibilities for it. I want board members to be aware of what they are signing up for, the influence that they have in the roles they have accepted, and the evolution of the patient population.

Board members are chosen for any number of reasons. However, the responsibility they have accepted is great, and the learning curve for many people not involved in healthcare in their daily lives is steep.

Although you may not have your hand in the everyday marketing decisions of your organization, you have just as much vested interest in marketing as those who do. Your opinions often influence marketing strategies, priorities, and budgets. I hope you find value, and some new perspectives, in the pages ahead.

WHY LISTEN TO ME?

With that in mind, you may be asking the question, "Who is Brandon Edwards, and why is he qualified to write a book on healthcare marketing?"

Fair question. I know you're eager to dive into the main ideas in the book. Before I do that, let me share a bit about my background and why I wrote this book so you have some additional context. I'll also share a quick roadmap of the book before we dive into Chapter One.

Authors write books for a wide variety of reasons. But when I considered this project, there were three main factors that compelled me to share my perspective on healthcare marketing.

First, I have worked directly in this industry for healthcare providers for thirty-one years. This is my life's work.

So much has happened in the last three decades. We've seen the death of the HMO era, broad introduction of electronic health records (EHR) use, the rise of the Affordable Care Act that made health insurance available to more people, and, more recently, the COVID era that has had such a huge impact on every facet of healthcare.

You never want to say, "I've seen it all." The minute we say that, something bizarre and unprecedented happens. At the same time, it's impossible to replace the wisdom and experience that comes from living through three decades of massive changes in healthcare.

Second, I'm the CEO of Unlock Health, the single largest and most effective marketing agency serving healthcare providers in the country. Before that, I was the CEO of the most awarded healthcare marketing agency in the history of healthcare marketing before we sold to Interpublic Group (IPG). These agencies have delivered services as agency of record, responsible for everything from brand strategy to measurement of ROI on service line campaigns. We've delivered this work across the integrated delivery network spectrum, from highly specialized academic medical centers to smaller rural health systems.

We were the "Best Agency to Work For" or "Agency of the Year" (or both) thirteen times in thirteen years. Some years, it was both—an accomplishment that made us the most awarded healthcare marketing agency in history.

I don't say all this to boast, but to boost your confidence in my experience and knowledge in the healthcare marketing space. In both organizations, I had the pleasure and experience to work with many of you or your predecessors.

Somewhere along the way in our journey of healthcare marketing, there was a compelling reason to pivot from what practices we had always used, to something very different. We are at that crossroads yet again, but on a global scale.

The third reason that compelled me to write this book is probably the most interesting one. I began my career working in crisis communications. Crises are almost always issues that have gone unaddressed or have not been taken seriously enough. Nothing teaches you about authentic marketing in the post-truth era quite like handling crises for healthcare providers. Most CMOs know this since they have responsibility for PR as well as marketing.

Working in crisis communications for a healthcare organization means you get to see what's happening in the healthcare system when things go wrong. And the reality is that *things always go wrong, and sometimes that means lives are lost.*

As you know, these are big, complex organizations with humans being treated by other humans, often with a common goal. Humans are complex and unpredictable creatures, and their perceived incentives may not be aligned. I've spent over three decades working in an industry where I've seen these realities up close and personal.

Many marketers don't see this "real" side of healthcare because the mistakes that happen in healthcare are often protected by attorney-client privilege or hidden behind a clinical peer-review process.

When you see what happens when things go wrong—and how it has a real effect on people's lives—it makes you more determined to get it right. It's why I'm so passionate about this topic.

As Larry Weber wrote in *Authentic Marketing*, "To be truly authentic, one essential element that *underlies everything* is making your brand more human and operating with more humanity. If you are genuine and good at the core, it will flow through every aspect of your business and reveal itself in everything you do."[4]

That is my goal for you, the reader, and all who are engaged in healthcare marketing—real, authentic marketing for the most important service we ever use in our lives.

I've asked my collaborator on this book, Shannon Hooper, to share a few words about her perspective on the topic of the book.

A WORD FROM SHANNON MCINTYRE HOOPER

I believe that, when done authentically, marketing can be the ultimate demonstration of curiosity and empathy—and that in the post-truth era, we have the responsibility to make it so.

---

4 Larry Weber, *Authentic Marketing: How to Capture Hearts and Minds Through the Power of Purpose* (Hoboken, NJ: Wiley, 2018), 101.

My own journey in this arena began after growing up in Georgia and heading to college in Connecticut. My studies landed at the intersection of political science, sociology, history, and religion. I became fascinated by the evolution of societal institutions and dogmatic belief systems. My senior thesis was originally intended to be a deep exploration of premillennial tradition in evangelical Christianity and a critique of its impact on regional and national politics.

And then, as I did my research, everything changed, and my thesis ended up being a critique on that critique. As I read through every piece of media coverage of the premillennial evangelical movement and countless political essays and books analyzing the topic, I was shocked by the vitriol of the media and the academy—the barely concealed hostility to these "backward believers" and the morally indignant attacks—not on their ways of thinking, but on *them*.

The divide between the left and right was alive and well, a step along the journey to today's post-truth era.

I didn't realize it at the time, but that year of research shaped more about what I stand for today than I could have imagined. I stand for an end to those polemics, and I believe that the only way to get there is to be a voyager into the hearts and minds of real people, to show genuine curiosity and demonstrate real understanding of how they arrived at their hard-won beliefs.

We have an incredible opportunity in healthcare to be a leader here. For hospitals in particular, there is a moral imperative to authentically reach all sorts of people and communities. This requires a complex balancing act: living an authentic brand positioning that finds the common ground while understanding the vastly diverse belief systems enough to deliver personalization that connects fully to individuals.

Authenticity is our only path to that dual mandate. And to get there, we must all challenge ourselves to find one another's humanity. Because judgment has no home for those trying to connect with and restore the health of our country.

THE ROAD AHEAD

Many thanks to Shannon for her invaluable contributions to this book.

My hope is that as you read Authentic Healthcare Marketing, you'll be inspired to act on what you are learning. To that end, I'm excited to take you on a journey where my goal is to inspire, challenge, and motivate you to drastically enhance your marketing.

I have chosen the metaphor of a journey to represent where we're headed. Marketing, especially in the field of healthcare, is a landscape where things are always changing. That's even more true these days, where change is happening at a faster pace than ever.

In **Chapters One and Two**, we'll explore the current moment we're in—the post-truth era—and explore why it creates such a challenge for healthcare marketing. We'll also unpack what "authentic" marketing looks and feels like.

This leads into **Chapters Three through Seven**, where I will explain the value of five key mile markers on the journey of authentic healthcare marketing. You'll understand why each of these is important and how to think about them in your organization.

Then in **Chapter Eight**, I will paint a picture of what success looks like for healthcare marketers, and share the next steps I advise you take on your marketing journey.

Here's the truth: If you keep doing what you've always been doing, you will miss out on connecting with a large portion of today's U.S. population. If you're a mission-driven organization, this reality should concern you.

I want you to come away from this book with absolute clarity that you need to adjust your marketing strategy and plans. In order to reach certain audiences in this post-truth era, your channels and messages need to be crafted to the nuances of this audience's preferences.

If you ignore this reality, you won't be as successful as you could be. You will compromise your mission. And most importantly, many people in your market will not receive the care they need.

This book is a call to action to rethink your marketing approach so you can effectively address our modern environment.

Thanks for spending some time with me as we explore what it means to market healthcare authentically. I know your time is valuable, so let's dive right in and get started by setting the context for what it means to live in our current post-truth era.

CHAPTER ONE

LIVING IN THE POST-TRUTH ERA

If there's one constant in life, it's *change.*

From the moment you are born until the moment you exit this life, you exist in a world where everything changes. Technology, relationships, power structures, and, yes, even our bodies are constantly evolving.

Just reflecting on the last two to three decades, the information has taken hold, we've seen the rise of e-commerce, an explosion of mobile phones over the traditional land line, and global shifts in commerce affecting the employment of millions of Americans.

In the last decade alone, major changes in the United States have happened with incredible speed. Venmo and PayPal are part of our daily transactions. Extreme weather events impact the availability of home insurance in our coastal communities. Social media dominates all our daily interactions and often, it seems, our very lives.

Additionally, a global pandemic has impacted the quality of our relationships—particularly among our children. We used to talk about BC and AD; now we talk about "before COVID" and "after COVID" because our lives changed so much in so short a period of time. In the post-COVID era, it's not unusual for people to feel like they're waking up in a world that didn't exist just a few years ago.

In our current climate, it's vital to understand that people get their information from all kinds of nontraditional sources, such as social media, influencers, podcasts, and heavily biased media sources, believed by audiences to be truthful and credible. The information landscape has consolidated to distinct ideological poles and left a huge gulf in the middle, with little shared worldview or even mutually recognized truths.

All this has created quite a challenge for healthcare organizations who want to reach and serve as many people as possible. Let's explore some of the features of the post-truth era, how it has impacted our view of traditional authority sources, and why this presents such a challenge for healthcare marketers.

WHAT IS THE POST-TRUTH ERA?

From time to time, you will hear someone say, "I know my truth," or, "That's not my truth." This perspective assumes there are different versions of the truth—that there is not a single "Big T" truth out there. This is just one symptom of the post-truth era.

We've been in this era for nearly twenty years. We can argue about when it began—some might say 9/11, and others might put the date perhaps a few years later, with the 2008 financial meltdown.

I believe this post-truth perspective became most apparent with the first Trump presidency in 2017. Keep in mind that I don't believe Trump caused it, nor is this intended to be an overtly political statement. His election was simply a reflection of society at the time, and since.

The 2016 election signaled a tipping point for our fundamental distrust of institutions, organizations, experts, and authorities that had been trusted for a long time. We relied on these entities to help us navigate our life more effectively and efficiently. No longer.

Times have changed. Today, many people don't listen to advice from traditional sources, such as financial advisors and healthcare experts. Instead, we listen to our echo chambers that reflect our own viewpoints.

RAND, a research organization, calls our current cultural malady "Truth Decay." RAND describes it as follows:

> Truth Decay is defined in part by an increasing disagreement about objective facts—a trend that exists on scale not observed in previous eras of American history. For example, despite having more evidence than ever before about vaccines being safe and effective at preventing disease, vaccine skepticism in the United States is on the rise.
>
> This is just one example of how public attitudes can diverge from facts and data in debates and discourse. So what's behind the decline?

> RAND researchers have identified four
> main drivers:
>
> 1. cognitive biases
> 2. changes to the information ecosystem,
>   including the rise of social media and
>   changes to the economics of news
> 3. demands on the educational system that
>   slow its ability to adapt to changes in
>   the information ecosystem
> 4. political and social polarization[5]

The rise of social media and its almost ubiquitous presence in our lives has only accelerated this dynamic. We see the same trend with cable news, where your entire worldview (no matter which side of the aisle you're on) is constantly validated by a selective reporting of facts that reinforce biases and sometimes outright untruths.

If advertisers and tech companies have discovered anything, it's that social media and the way that we talk about these issues in general are incredible rage generators … and, therefore, revenue generators. For them, rage equals engagement, and engagement equals marketing dollars.

Marketers have understood this for a long time. It takes ten positives to overcome every negative. Anger, rage, and mistrust are extremely powerful motivators in human behavior. Sadly, they are rarely constructive influences in the healthcare system.

I experienced this personally in 2013 when my mother passed away. It's not as if she suddenly became sick and died.

---

5 RAND Corporation, "About Truth Decay," last modified January 16, 2018, https://www.rand.org/research/projects/truth-decay/about-truth-decay.html

We had many disagreements and discussions about the healthcare alternatives available to her and the care choices that she'd made for years before that. I just never won any of those arguments.

This isn't just an academic or theoretical issue. When we make poor choices, we end up at the small rural community hospital instead of Stanford for specialized care, or we end up pursuing unproven treatments instead of ones based in real medical expertise and science.

We make decisions about our health every single day in hundreds of ways. Our eating and sleeping habits play a critical role in our health, and so do our decisions regarding when and where to receive care.

For many people, a local urgent care is sufficient for treating bumps and bruises. On the flip side, many people will seek an academic medical center like Stanford for highly specialized care after a cancer diagnosis.

In the middle of those two scenarios, for everything from annual checkups to orthopedic surgeries to hospice care and more, the consumer is now barraged with a litany of choices of where and when to seek care.

Making a good choice here can, quite literally, save your life. Yet we rely increasingly on word of mouth and the restrictions imposed by health insurance and decreasingly on the recommendation of clinicians, which opens the door for us to make poor choices or to pursue quackery treatments instead of real medical expertise.

Truthful, Authentic Healthcare Marketing should help people find what they need, guide them to their appropriate next steps, and provide them with objective decision-making criteria along the way.

When you zoom out and look at mistrust in traditional healthcare expertise on a society-wide level, it has a chilling impact. When you have a million deaths outside the normal, predictable mortality patterns in the United States, as we did with COVID, it has a material impact on the entire economy.

For example, it affects senior living operators, pharmaceutical companies, and healthcare providers who might have expected some of those older patients to need future care. And that's just a few ways that a pandemic can affect our economy. We can also talk about the myriad other ways something like this impacts our lives.

If I refuse to be vaccinated, for example, maybe I think it's not a big deal because I think I'm the only one who might get sick. But if I don't get a polio or measles vaccine, or any of these other vaccines, that has the potential to impact my community in a consequential way.

The post-truth era has an effect on every level of society, of course, but for healthcare, it's much more significant. It can mean the difference between life and death.

Let's consider the dynamics of why traditional sources of authority have faded and what has taken their place.

THE EROSION OF TRADITIONAL AUTHORITY

This process begins with what a person believes. Those beliefs manifest into choices, which lead to certain possible behaviors.

In large part, people have come to believe certain things about healthcare that are inaccurate. But it doesn't just begin and end with healthcare. These beliefs begin with other industries that have a huge impact on our health—for example, the food industry.

If there's one thing that's profoundly dysfunctional in the United States, it's how we think about food, how we consume it, and how we produce and market it. One of the best illustrations of this is Morgan Spurlock's 2004 documentary, *Super Size Me.*

In the film, Spurlock goes through a period of time eating only at McDonald's, and his rule was that any time a larger option was offered, he took it. At the end of the period, his health markers showed significant decline. The point was clear.

We are allowed to do things in our country that aren't allowed in many other developed countries. For example, we subsidize certain foods that are demonstrably unhealthy, and the resulting disproportionate consumption of these products has led to record obesity rates. Then you have all the other industries that spring up to address that problem—the healthcare, diet, and fitness industries, just to name a few. It takes concerted efforts by conscientious leaders to address these issues. As CEO of PepsiCo, Indra Nooyi made tremendous changes to the company and its sugar products sold in schools out of a recognition of the impact they were having on school-aged children.

Despite these examples, consumers still refuse to seek out truth, facts, and science. Our base needs and wants to overcome our critical abilities, and the system ensures this cycle continues in terms of food marketing, government subsidies, and everything else that shapes what we eat and how we think about nutrition. What other possible reason could someone give for all the unhealthy behaviors and disregard for basic nutrition that we have in our country?

Another example: If you ask people how they choose their doctors, the single greatest factor is a recommendation from friends or family. Yet why do we assume that our friends and family know anything about how to evaluate doctors or hospitals?

Perhaps this also reveals a fundamental failure of the industry to communicate health-related details to patients in layperson terms, or to provide tools for people to make useful decisions about their healthcare.

Part of the reason people don't understand the difference in providers is because we don't have a standard definition of quality and service. We certainly don't have any useful tools to understand the price we will pay out of pocket, or what our health insurance pays, for healthcare services.

There's an old joke in the healthcare industry: "There are a thousand top 100 hospitals." This joke exists because there are fourteen organizations that rank hospitals on different criteria, most of which are poorly understood. I honestly don't even know if this is strictly true, but we all know it's directionally true. To quote the villain Syndrome in the Incredibles movie, "Everyone can be super. And when everyone's super, no one will be."

Believing the wrong thing is bad enough. But when you compound misplaced beliefs with irreversible choices, the results can be catastrophic.

That is why any journey toward authentic healthcare marketing must begin with helping people know and believe the right things, make better choices, and ultimately have better behaviors.

THREE CHALLENGES FACING HEALTHCARE MARKETERS

Nobody said this would be easy, though. Our post-truth era presents three significant challenges for those of us who want to reach our communities with high-quality, accessible healthcare and to serve them well.

The first challenge is to create messaging for *people who mistrust institutions and "experts."*

The main problem with hospitals and health systems when it comes to marketing is that they are a place, an institution. In the post-truth era, what do we distrust? Institutions, especially big ones.

As a result, hospitals highlight their doctors. In marketing, you see a lot of experts in white coats who represent an institution. When COVID first emerged, experts were sought out to inform us and help us understand the magnitude of the situation. When crafting health system communications, we identified physicians and researchers in the CDC as the most believable spokespersons. They held far more trust than hospital administrators or politicians. Yet in the past few years, people have decided to distrust experts almost as much as institutions. Then we wonder why people aren't listening.

That's why we have to figure out how to share health information with people who may not know how to hear it, to provide it exactly when they need it, and to do so in a credible way.

This crisis of credibility presents a fantastic opportunity to learn from other marketing campaigns that have used perceived flaws to actually improve credibility.

Take the classic Volkswagen "Lemon" ad from 1960. As part of the "Think Small" campaign for the Volkswagen Beetle, it showed a black-and-white image of a Beetle with a single word in bold underneath: "Lemon."

Lemon.

This Volkswagen missed the boat.

The chrome strip on the glove compartment is blemished and must be replaced. Chances are you wouldn't have noticed it; Inspector Kurt Kroner did.

There are 3,389 men at our Wolfsburg factory with only one job: to inspect Volkswagens at each stage of production. (3000 Volkswagens are produced daily; there are more inspectors than cars.)

Every shock absorber is tested (spot checking won't do), every windshield is scanned. VWs have been rejected for surface scratches barely visible to the eye.

Final inspection is really something! VW inspectors run each car off the line onto the Funktionsprüfstand (car test stand), tote up 189 check points, gun ahead to the automatic brake stand, and say "no" to one VW out of fifty.

This preoccupation with detail means the VW lasts longer and requires less maintenance, by and large, than other cars. (It also means a used VW depreciates less than any other car.)

We pluck the lemons; you get the plums.

ONE OF THE BEST AND MOST AUTHENTIC ADVERTISEMENTS EVER.

The text of the ad explained that this particular car had been rejected because of a tiny blemish, thereby highlighting Volkswagen's strict quality control standards. By calling out one of its rare "lemons" from the production line, the company reassured potential customers they could expect a high level of quality from Volkswagen. They also showed a sense of humor—a quality sorely lacking in most marketing.

It's difficult to imagine a healthcare organization running an ad this honest, and yet that's the point, isn't it? Traditional healthcare marketing presents a polished, perfect picture ... and no one believes it.

The second challenge is understanding that *people access information in different ways than the past.*

Historically, we would have said that hospital marketing tends to trail general marketing strategies and trends by five to ten years. That gap has narrowed somewhat in recent years, but what we're seeing now is that people are consuming information about health and healthcare providers largely from social media, word of mouth, and influencers.

What does that mean in practice? That we are often huddled in polarized echo chambers. It means everyone's views are constantly being validated, even if those views are inaccurate, because there is always some segment of the population that believes the same as you. We naturally seek out the places that resonate with our beliefs—and get nothing but recurring validation there.

It's a huge challenge for healthcare marketers because they have to be much more present and engaged with audiences across the social media spectrum—the very place where there can be a cesspool of misinformation, post-truth fake news, and all manner of extreme and uninformed viewpoints.

Marketers must change where and how they show up and be willing to lean into really uncomfortable channels and discussions so they can meet people where they are. In choosing to reach out across these audiences, we have to consider some of the reasons that people are there to begin with. Perhaps they enjoy the entertainment value or the aggressiveness inherent in the interactions more than the factual accuracy.

If our goal is to plant seeds in the minds of our audience, we might need to accommodate changes in our messaging to first gain mindshare, and then move toward "real" truths. I acknowledge this is tough to swallow, but it's absolutely essential to consider.

I remember Ty Webb, Chevy Chase's character in *Caddyshack*, saying, "In one physical model of the universe, the shortest distance between two points is a straight line—in the opposite direction." As against the grain as that may seem, that's the direction many of us in marketing need to go.

The third challenge is connecting with *people who are more disconnected from each other than ever before.*

The biggest irony of social media can be illustrated by a single image of a family sitting together in the same room. None of them are conversing with anyone in the room because they are all glued to their phones.

This is true not only on the level of family units, but society as well. We are more connected than ever, while at the same time we are also more isolated, lonely, and disconnected from each other. Is it the isolation aspect of disconnection that keeps marketers from connecting with their audiences? Or is it the lack of conversation and real communication between people resulting from this disconnection that hinders us? Perhaps these are one in the same.

This disconnection comes with a price. As Ralph Keyes writes in *The Post-Truth Era:*

> When it comes to post-truthfulness, the fraying of human connections is both cause and effect. Not feeling connected to others makes it easier to lie, which in turn makes it harder to reconnect. Eroded communities foster dishonesty. Dishonesty contributes to the further erosion of communities.[6]

The dishonesty that comes as a result of disconnection manifests itself in a hundred different ways, including a mistrust of traditional authorities and experts, and a turn toward alternative sources of information.

Given all these realities, how do we proceed? What can marketers in healthcare do to help their organizations achieve their mission of reaching people who need care?

The answer lies in approaching our marketing authentically. That's what the next chapter is all about.

---

6 Ralph Keyes, The Post-Truth Era: Dishonesty and Deception in Contemporary Life (New York: St. Martin's Press, 2004), 41.

CHAPTER TWO

WHY WE NEED AUTHENTIC HEALTHCARE MARKETING

I hope that Chapter One has helped you see that the realities of our post-truth era have made effective healthcare marketing more important than ever.

As the title of this book indicates, I believe the answer isn't more creative or clever marketing—it's more *authentic* marketing.

Creativity is essential, and cleverness is a bonus when a company seeks to make a connection. But what does *authentic* mean specifically? Why is it so important to look at marketing this way? How do you measure it?

In this chapter, I'll answer those questions and more. These will then lead us into the five mile markers we will explore beginning in the next chapter.

WHAT IS AUTHENTIC HEALTHCARE MARKETING?

Let's return to the definition of Authentic Healthcare Marketing that I shared earlier and unpack it.

Authentic Healthcare Marketing is the process of communicating a healthcare brand's key messaging that is rooted in your mission, values, and strategy and helps the right audience connect with, believe in, and trust your message.

Let's break this definition down into its component parts.

First, let's discuss identifying the "right audience." Obviously, one of the basics of marketing communication is to identify the right audience; to make sure the right messages are getting to the right people in the right places. However, in our discussion around authenticity, there is a higher bar. The message and the channel it's delivered through need to be authentic, too. This isn't just getting the message and medium right; it's getting the tone, the language, the visual style, and, above all, the connection right, too.

For instance, an orthopedic message about knee pain or a message about flu shots may be trying to get a response from its audience (such as following a call to action [CTA] to finding out more about orthopedics, or getting a flu shot), but the stimulus needed to get that response is likely to be very different across age, geography, gender, social milieu, and so on. Marketing communication that speaks to twentysomethings may bear little tonal, visual, or linguistic resemblance to something that speaks to seventy-somethings. That is what meeting your audience where they are entails.

The second characteristic of Authentic Healthcare Marketing is that the message is something the audience can "connect with, believe in, and trust." How do we connect in an authentic way to our audience? I've given considerable thought to what really constitutes "authenticity" in the context of healthcare marketing and have developed four key dimensions of authenticity. These dimensions force us to focus on the consumer/patient/target perspective mindset and come at our work through their lens. It forces us to think about our output from the perspective of people caught in the post-truth world, unsure of what and whom to trust.

MOST USEFUL SOURCE OF HOSPITAL INFORMATION IN DECISION-MAKING

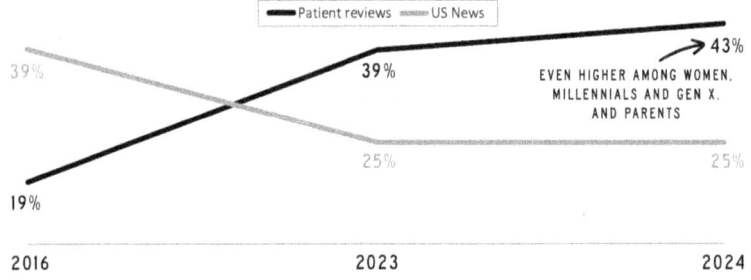

All too often we are thinking about satisfying our internal audiences—the people with the decision-making power over our campaigns. Part of being authentic in our work is focusing on the audience who is *consuming* our work, not just those approving it or making it happen. After all, if we are successful at wooing our intended audience, the C-suite executives will likely be happy as well.

At Unlock Health, we use a tool called The Healthcare Authenticity Index which measures the four dimensions of authenticity for consumers. They are as follows:

- "Does it speak a human truth to our audience?"
- "Is it meaningful for our audience?"

- "Is it believable?"
- "Can our audience trust this?"

These dimensions can inform and inspire work. They can also be used to judge and evaluate work, and ultimately can be used to measure how authentic the audience believes the work to be.

We use them every day in our work as a formal reminder to advocate for these dimensions with our clients and encourage them to use them as well.

Third, the use of "message" is more of a proxy word for a number of outputs. It could be a brand, some content, a website, etc. We have used "message" to simplify our mission statement.

Finally, let's discuss messaging that is rooted in your mission, values, and strategy. I feel strongly that being authentic to the audience is only one side of the coin. Any organization could be authentic in the eyes of the audience, but is it still being authentic to itself? We all know people who have a chameleon-like ability to adapt to whomever they are talking to, but these people lack a clear sense of self. No company is everything to everyone. A clear sense of your mission, values, and strategy will help your audience understand why you are right for them.

For me, the person or organization sending the message needs a clear sense of self, purpose, and direction. The best place to find these things should be in an organization's mission, vision, values, and strategy. Ideally, these elements are a North Star for any organization, and marketing communications will be more successful if they are informed by these elements.

TWO IMPORTANT DIMENSIONS

When I look at our client organizations, I think about adding two dimensions to ensure work is authentic to the organization it's coming from.

- "Does it reflect our mission, vision, and values?"
- "Is it in alignment with our strategy?"

By contrast, inauthentic marketing is advertising conducted in a way that doesn't reflect the organization's mission and values, or it leads people to believe things that are untrue to accomplish a self-serving goal.

Inauthentic marketing fails to connect with people, fails to deliver meaning, and fails to create trust. To give a general example: If a faith-based organization put out an advertisement that was crass or contained inappropriate sexual humor, that would be inauthentic.

Authentic Healthcare Marketing also has to be accurate and truthful. You can't say whatever you want. We must hold ourselves to a higher standard in healthcare. It doesn't mean we have to share "the entire truth" with someone (e.g., you can't share all information with all people). Yet it means that everything we say must be truthful.

Look at the words in your messaging and judge whether they are truthful and real. Can you validate that your message is true and accurate? Sounds simple, but in our post-truth era this simple test has become surprisingly rare. You have to set an anchor in two different places: your organization's mission and the audience's beliefs.

Authentic Healthcare Marketing also blends the head and the heart. I'll share a common understanding from the healthcare marketing world. If you're the faith-based hospital, you're going to appeal to people's hearts. Your marketing is likely emotionally driven, and people will assume you're not as technologically advanced as your competitors.

If you're a secular hospital, you'll likely highlight your equipment and technology. People will assume you are clinically advanced but cold and less empathetic than your faith-based competitors. This is also validated in all public opinion research.

Neither of these stereotypes is wholly true, of course, and so marketing that leans into these and inaccuracies is not truly authentic.

The reality is that good marketing needs to blend both the head (facts) and heart (emotions). Authentic marketing strives to always finds the balance.

It is important that we get this right because healthcare is very important in people's lives. We need to connect with people not just factually but also emotionally. People tend to base emergency room (ER) decisions largely on emotional engagement and proximity. Their choice of a primary care provider (PCP) is more factually driven, but they do tend to have a requirement for an emotional connection with their PCP. Specialists are a blend of the two decision-making styles, requiring a mix of geographic proximity, competency evaluation, and emotional connection.

Meeting people's needs by providing the type of information they want is part of what drives resonance (e.g., including location when advertising an ER clinic). People are not robots. We respond to both types of persuasion.

It's all about clearly identifying your mission and purpose, then tying your marketing to that. You shouldn't have to guess at what these things are. In healthcare, we know what we're trying to accomplish. Authentic marketing connects the essence of your organization to the real consumer or patient on the other end, with all their biases.

In the United States, more than 50 percent of hospitals are nonprofit, and less than 20 percent are faith-based. Each knows their respective mission and values, albeit many sound the same and often lack differentiation.

The challenge comes when marketers struggle to connect the mission to people's lives and what they really care about. You have to bring the organization's mission and values to life in a way that furthers the mission but also serves the business purpose.

Of course, we have to start with an analysis of the organization's mission and values to determine their authenticity—i.e., to make sure they are truly specific to the organization. If they could apply to any organization, they are not authentic enough.

WHY AUTHENTICITY MATTERS

Of course, it has always been important for marketers to connect with the mission, purpose, and values of an organization. That's nothing new.

So why is authenticity more important than ever? There are three answers.

First, in a world where everything seems to be fake and manufactured, people are rewarded for being authentic. Reward doesn't mean everyone agrees with you, but you will convert some nonbelievers, and you will cement your credibility with people who are open to connecting with you.

People who show up as their authentic selves, even when that authenticity is not so likable or positive, draw others to them. The same is true for brands, institutions, and organizations. People can sense when something isn't authentic.

Second, healthcare marketing is a value driver, not simply a cost center. While this isn't a book about healthcare finance or formulas for profitability, I would be remiss if I did not point out that we do need to make a profit. Many healthcare CEOs and CFOs view marketing as an expense, not an investment. When it is done well, from an authentic place, healthcare marketing fulfills our mission of connecting people to the care they need, when they need it most, which translates to revenue for our C-suite friends. Without successful healthcare marketing, most organizations will fail.

Third, it's very easy to say whatever you want to get people's attention. Today, we have a greater tolerance than ever for untruths and inaccuracies. Is it tolerance or willful acceptance? It feels like a substantial portion of the U.S. population is willing to go along with falsity in order to escape their present reality. Sometimes, I sympathize.

However, I believe that in healthcare, we have an obligation to do better. We can't follow the "ends justify the means" rationale.

We can't say that we're all about good science, saving people's lives, and improving the world, and then speak in a way that is inauthentic or not factual.

Just because other people, entities, or institutions are being inauthentic and getting great results does not give us the right to do it as well. Don't be drawn into that way of operating. Stay true to your principles, and you will win in the long run.

In *Authentic Marketing*, Larry Weber encourages all marketers to take the high road:

> As these core components come together—a business strategy fueled by moral purpose, use of technology innovations to elevate customer experience, and efforts to solve a problem in the world—they provide great fodder for genuine, transparent, and meaningful stories that can forge positive connections to the brand.

> Stories of a company's moral purpose, in particular, will be the purest form of authentic marketing. When a company does genuine good for the world, constituents will immediately recognize the authenticity in those stories, prompting them to like and share them, and perhaps tell their own experiences with the brand. This is the most powerful form of marketing a company can experience, as it demonstrates how customers can serve to co-create brand.[7]

All this might seem like theory when you consider the details of your actual job. But it's where we must begin if we are to rise above what everyone else in our industry is doing.

Thinking about authenticity has paid off in other sectors. We know that authentic brands can be admired, loved, and financially successful. This model is also sustainable. Authentic brands aren't fashionable or a flash in the pan—and if they are, it's not of their doing! They are classic—evergreens that stand the test of time because they are authentic to their core.

It's worth taking a look at Authenticity 500 (https://www. authenticity.co). This is a ranking of the world's most authentic brands. Number One is Patagonia.

Patagonia was built on Yvon Chouinard's love of climbing. At fourteen he became a member of the Southern California Falconry Club, rappelling down the cliffs to the falcon aeries. As a seventeen-year-old, he taught himself how to blacksmith and started making pitons. Eight years later he formed a partnership to make climbing equipment.

---

7 Weber, Authentic Marketing, 56.

In the early 1970s he started to sell clothing for climbing. A combination of innovation and environmental and social justice has fueled the brand ever since. In 2022, Yvon put 100 percent of the company's voting stock in a trust to protect the company's values and 100 percent of the nonvoting stock into a nonprofit dedicated to fighting the environmental crisis and defending nature. Each year, money made after reinvesting in the business is distributed to fund efforts to save the planet.

Yvon writes, "Earth is now our only shareholder."[8] The origin story rings true, as does the business model. The quality and consistency of the products as well as the company's commitment to its core values makes Patagonia a global icon for authenticity. In financial terms, Patagonia is not a huge company compared with most healthcare organizations, yet its brand is known throughout the world.

I believe there should be a brand known for its authenticity in healthcare. The sector lends itself to it.

HOW TO MEASURE AUTHENTICITY

If authenticity is so important, how do we measure or validate it? Is there a way to know if we are achieving it? How can we know if we are being authentic in our marketing?

There is an argument to be made that public opinion research or analytics can uncover how people feel about your brand. You can ask some fairly straightforward questions, such as, "Does Vanderbilt Health care about me as a person?" and "Do they deliver information I find credible and useful?"

You can track those responses over time, using one of the mainstream tracking services just like many organizations do. This

---

8   Brian Trelstad et al., "Patagonia: 'Earth Is Now Our Only Shareholder,'" Harvard Business School Case 323-057, March 2023, revised September 2023, https://www.hbs.edu/faculty/Pages/item.aspx?num=63834

can tell you whether the perception of your brand is improving or declining over time.

However, those kind of metrics will not necessarily help you understand if your brand is seen as authentic. Useful? Excellent? Recognized? Perhaps. But authenticity is different.

Earlier in this chapter, I mentioned The Healthcare Authenticity Index. This tool measures how authentic any work of marketing communication is. I'll repeat the four dimensions here to drive home the point:

- "Does it speak a human truth to our audience?"
- "Is it meaningful for our audience?"
- "Is it believable?"
- "Can our audience trust this?"

When we work with organizations to improve their marketing, we can create a measurement tool that starts with these questions and build out a campaign, brand, or messaging benchmark from there, or we can append these questions to an existing survey. They are simple, effective, and easy to deploy.

Over time, we build up a rich database that we can use for benchmarks that can help us derive principles for creating authentic work.

THE ROLE OF TRANSPARENCY

I would be remiss if I did not talk about one of the most pressing issues when it comes to authenticity—a lack of transparency in the financial aspect of healthcare.

I will begin by pointing out that hospitals and health systems actually have a fair amount of financial transparency about their overall performance because most of them are nonprofit organizations. As such, they have a legal obligation to make their financial records public.

That type of transparency is not what the typical patient cares about, though. They are often frustrated at the lack of transparency around how much they have to pay out of pocket for healthcare services. It is frequently stated that U.S. healthcare is the only industry that allows us to buy a service or product without knowing what that service costs up front.

A huge part of people's decision-making about where to receive care, and what kind of care they receive (or don't receive), comes down to whether they can afford it. Will my insurance cover this provider or procedure? Are they in network?

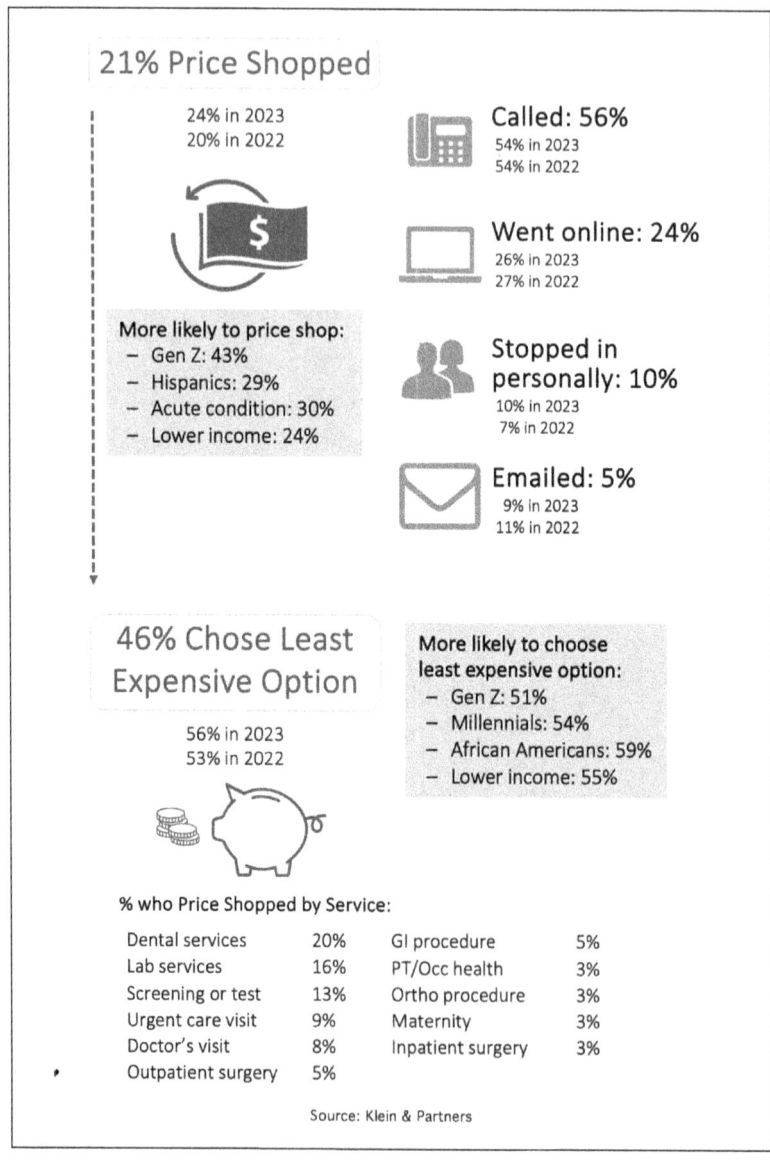

21% Price Shopped

24% in 2023
20% in 2022

More likely to price shop:
- Gen Z: 43%
- Hispanics: 29%
- Acute condition: 30%
- Lower income: 24%

Called: 56%
54% in 2023
54% in 2022

Went online: 24%
26% in 2023
27% in 2022

Stopped in personally: 10%
10% in 2023
7% in 2022

Emailed: 5%
9% in 2023
11% in 2022

46% Chose Least Expensive Option

56% in 2023
53% in 2022

More likely to choose least expensive option:
- Gen Z: 51%
- Millennials: 54%
- African Americans: 59%
- Lower income: 55%

% who Price Shopped by Service:

Service	%	Service	%
Dental services	20%	GI procedure	5%
Lab services	16%	PT/Occ health	3%
Screening or test	13%	Ortho procedure	3%
Urgent care visit	9%	Maternity	3%
Doctor's visit	8%	Inpatient surgery	3%
Outpatient surgery	5%		

Source: Klein & Partners

Any healthcare provider, doctor, hospital, or group that genuinely cares about people must, by definition, care about whether those people are making informed choices. Price estimating tools may be difficult to install and sometimes produce inaccurate data, but we must try. It must be a priority because the true owner of this information, the health insurance payor, has refused to do so. Thus, it is left to those with a mission and purpose of caring for others to inform them of the costs of care.

People's choices are informed by the answers to the questions *What is this going to cost me?* and *Can I even afford this?*

Many health systems deal with this by presenting the standard line, "Our prices don't really matter. We take care of people no matter what, regardless of their financial situation." That may be true from a mission and policy standpoint, but it's almost never true in a macro sense or to the individual. We can and should do better.

There is a huge gap in credibility when a hospital says, "We take care of anybody who needs it," but they present you with a gigantic bill. If you can't pay, maybe they will write it off, or maybe they will give you a discount or apply their charity care policy. Worse, they could pursue medical debt collection, which is the number one cause of bankruptcy in the United States.[9]

Yet your customers don't know how you're going to respond to financial issues before they use your services. That's a problem that affects people's lives, affects access to the healthcare system, and affects the brand of every hospital and health system—even though, in many cases, providing this information accurately is the responsibility of the insurer.

Healthcare is unlike any other industry in the world. To buy a $50,000 car, we have our credit checked to be approved for a bank loan. If we have a mechanic assess the problems with this car, they provide an estimate of repair costs, detailing what will

---

9 Jennifer Streaks, "Medical Bankruptcy: What It Is, What It Means, and Why It's So Common in the United States," *Business Insider*, September 16, 2024, https://www.businessinsider.com/personal-finance/credit-score/medical-bankruptcies

be required and the cost. We decide what needs to be done based on the seriousness and affordability.

If hospitals truly care about helping people, wouldn't they make sure they didn't allow the patient to choose something that is going to destroy them financially? Wouldn't they make sure the patient is making an informed decision? Or is the mission to care for the physical condition of the patient at the expense of their entire well-being? Wouldn't the insurer and the employer do the same?

I understand that this line of thinking is hard to integrate into operations. It's easy to blame insurance companies for the mess we're in when it comes to healthcare costs. But there are many other factors at work.

Yet it also doesn't release the hospital or healthcare provider from being transparent and authentic. Even if we can't solve the problem with 100 percent accurate and timely estimates before care is provided, we can talk about these financial issues more.

How? We can empathize with what people are dealing with. And we can make it a little bit easier to determine financial impacts, even if the results aren't perfect. That would do more to build trust in the average health system's brand than almost anything else you could do.

Most hospitals shy away from talking about anything related to finances. My impression is that most are uncomfortable with the subject and perceive that the prices they charge for services is incongruent with their mission to help people. Chargemasters and the rates we charge health insurance companies for the care we provide their members can be complex and tough to understand.

The problem is that this lack of pricing transparency really leaves people in limbo. They don't know what decisions to make, what their care is going to cost them, or, in many cases, whether they are going to be financially devastated by the cost of care.

The reality is that there is so much about the healthcare system that is not optimally designed from a financial standpoint. There are many good and practical reasons why hospitals do what they do. They don't love this system any more than anyone else does, but they still have to be financially sustainable. After all, doctors, equipment, and a thousand other things cost money.

GETTING THE JOB DONE

How do we put the concepts from this chapter into practice? It's one thing to talk about theories and debate issues in healthcare. When push comes to shove, we have to get the job done.

The good news is that we are not just using an insignificant tool to get the job done. We're using the most important aspect of great marketing—authenticity.

Seth Godin shed a bit of insight into this great power in his book *All Marketers Are Liars*:

> I believe marketing is the most powerful force available to people who want to make change. And with that power comes responsibility. We (anyone with the ability to tell a story—online, in print or to the people in our communities) have the ability to change things more dramatically than ever before in history.[10]

Remember, you're not just a marketer. You're a powerful communicator with the ability to change people's hearts and minds. What you do matters.

---

10 Seth Godin, *All Marketers Are Liars* (New York: Portfolio), 20.

I believe that healthcare marketing communication is, in and of itself, a form of healthcare. COVID proved that beyond all doubt. The communication about diseases and health conditions, what to watch out for, getting vaccinations, screenings, and other preventative care are all examples of how marketing communications in their own right are instruments of healthcare.

I'll be the first to admit that we have focused on some grim realities of the healthcare industry in this chapter. Rob Klein, of the healthcare research firm Klein & Partners, put it well:

> "Healthcare has become a low-attention category. People don't take as much time to be choosy with their healthcare as they used to. They want to know if a brand can give them the care they need, when, where, how and with whom they want it. And they want to be able to trust the messenger."[11]

---

11 Rob Klein, unpublished white paper (March 7, 2025), provided to the author.

AVERAGE TRUST RATING
(2024)

0   6.19   10

6.38 in 2023
6.45 in 2022
Pre-COVID   6.12 in 2019
5.44 in 2015

	Do not trust them at all								Trust them completely		2023	2022	Pre-COVID	
	0	1	2	3	4	5	6	7	8	9	10			2019	2015
Children's Hospitals									7.77			7.47	7.44	7.35	7.04
Physicians									7.55			7.39	7.34	7.20	6.69
University Hospitals (Teaching/ Academic)								6.92				6.89	6.92	6.90	6.05
Non-profit hospitals								6.88				6.81	6.84	6.83	6.19
CVS							6.47					6.54	6.68	NA	NA
WebMD							6.23					6.44	6.38	6.22	NA
Google							6.08					6.28	6.24	5.75	NA
US News & World Report Hospital Rankings						5.92						5.93	6.00	6.74	NA
Amazon						5.82						6.22	6.37	5.75	NA
For-profit hospitals						5.70						5.87	6.20	5.82	4.95
Walmart						5.63						5.97	5.89	NA	NA
Health insurance companies						5.53						5.98	6.16	5.32	3.77
Apple						5.32						5.96	5.96	5.07	NA
Pharmaceutical companies					4.84							5.60	5.78	4.52	3.37

Source: Klein & Partners

Rob's insights lay the perfect foundation for asking the question, "What should we do?" I'll answer that question in various ways, and with many details and specifics, throughout the rest of this book.

However, before we dive into the mile markers in the pages ahead, I want to emphasize one of the most critical factors in any successful healthcare marketing campaign. Let me explain.

Agencies like to make things. Clients like to receive things. Many people in healthcare marketing like to see something tangible before providing feedback. But by then it may be too late. We may have already missed the chance to set the table in the way that gives us the best chance for a successful outcome.

One of the most crucial things we can do is to agree with all parties in the process of developing authentic healthcare marketing about exactly what that means and what it takes to do it. Because it does take more commitment than just creating a marketing campaign that makes it into the world.

Let's go back to our definition:

Authentic Healthcare Marketing is the process of communicating a healthcare brand's key messaging that is rooted in your mission, values, and strategy and helps the right audience connect with, believe in, and trust your message.

Committing to authentic marketing is a healthcare win-win. For all parties signing up to do this, it means sticking to it. For the owners of the mission, values, and strategy, it means staying true to those elements. For the creators of the marketing communications, it means not settling for anything less than what has been agreed to. For the engaged audience, it means getting the care they need.

The implications of all parties signing up to this commitment are significant. Marketing communications will become more effective because they will resonate better with the target audience. The reputation of the client organization should be more coherent and cohesive because marketing communications will always link back to the mission, values, and strategy. And marketing communication campaigns will yield better results because they will be more meaningful to their audiences.

With that foundation, I'm now going to share with you the five mile markers of Authentic Healthcare Marketing. To begin, let's take a look at the first one, Authentic Insights.

CHAPTER THREE

MILE MARKER #1— AUTHENTIC INSIGHTS

By this point in the book, I hope I have persuaded you to do the work it takes to make your marketing authentic. That will mean a variety of things to different organizations, as the specifics can vary wildly. Let's start our journey by exploring the first mile marker: Authentic Insights.

A wise ex-Ogilvy strategist, Beth Barry, once said there are "sights" and "insights." *Sights* are simply observations. *Insights*, on the other hand, change how you see something to the point where you will always view it in that new way and never unsee it. She added, "Don't confuse the two."

Another definition of a true insight is "an undiscovered cliché." After all, when first coined, phrases that become cliché are so novel and true that they spread like wildfire in our collective vocabularies. Authentic insights are rare and powerful. They are worth hunting down because they are game-changing.

The best way to unearth authentic insights to share with your audience is through the use of analytics and research. This can feel intimidating to people who aren't naturally geared toward numbers, statistics, or research. Don't feel intimidated, though.

My purpose here isn't to give you all the details (that would constitute a book many times this size), but rather to share a new way for you to think about your marketing.

At its broadest level, analytics and research can help you better understand and uncover authentic insights about the market and your place in it, understand your consumers' and patients' preferences, predict marketing impacts, execute a targeted and effective marketing campaign, and measure the achievement of that campaign against those impacts. Let's break this down a little further.

As a reader of this book, you are probably in healthcare marketing or healthcare. Even if you operate in the same field or have the same role as someone else, you are still competing in a slightly different market.

That's because no two organizations are exactly alike. There is variance in geography and competencies. Further, the level of competition varies from urban to rural areas. The scope and strength of services offered by each system or hospital vary, and that is reflected in the brand strength and influences consumer preferences. A given organization's share of their market in service offerings tends to align with consumer perception, so this can serve as an indicator of how authentic our messaging regarding each service offering is perceived in the market.

Analytics and research also help you deeply understand your audiences—those you think you know, and those cloaked by the "closed communities" endemic in the post-truth era. Analytics and research help you map your messages and approach to your actual audience.

Knowing where we stand in the market and in the eyes of our consumers, we can start to use historical marketing efforts as a guide toward predicting how likely we are to achieve our mission-focused marketing goals with our current programming and budget.

For example, offering ourselves as a better alternative for a knee replacement than a competitor that has invested in and marketed its orthopedic excellence and is well regarded might take a lot more effort than improving our market share in other services. We may also already have captured significant commercial market share paid at a rate well above the market.

Lastly, once we choose a course of action, select an audience, and put our messaging out across deliberately selected channels, we want to know how our investment is performing. Measurement is the most widely perceived use of analytics in healthcare marketing today. This is where the rubber meets the road in our journey, and when we learn how well our plans achieve the goals we set out to accomplish.

When you think about the use of analytics and research, it's about how you need to think about, and plan, your work. We're not trying to show what a detailed marketing campaign looks like, but rather focus on the thinking behind it. Let's begin by thinking about why analytics and research matter in the first place—in fact, now more than ever before.

MORE IMPORTANT THAN EVER

One of the big markers of our post-truth era is that people's opinions have the same weight, the same validity, as actual facts. But in healthcare, certain things are just *facts*. They are not debatable.

For example, getting a colonoscopy at a certain age is going to reduce your chances of developing terminal cancer by a certain percentage. I could cite many other examples where prevention, screenings, and early detection are going to help you stay healthier and live longer.

These are facts. It's not just a matter of *these healthcare providers are trying to get me to do this or that.*

We can argue if you're better off having a colonoscopy at age forty, forty-five, or fifty given the occasional changes in the standard set by the experts. That is a legitimate conversation to have. Yet no one can legitimately argue that you're better off not having a colonoscopy or that colonoscopies are somehow harmful. That's where opinions start to run headlong into facts and science.

We are talking about the presentation of facts to an audience. Those facts should be able to be independently validated by research and clinical experts.

In healthcare, we tend to emphasize the facts about healthcare when we talk to audiences instead of conveying that we understand their broader worldview. If I know how you feel about a variety of other topics, that information will help me develop a better profile of you so that I can communicate with you effectively.

Audience segmentation and effective message targeting is possible when we heed the research, use analytics to reveal everything we can about the people we serve, and accept that we cannot speak to all audiences with the same voice and the same messages.

Analytics is not just about socioeconomic demographics, but also psychographics—how people think. For example, about 12 percent of the U.S. population believes the moon landings were fake. About 10 percent of the population believes the world is flat. Those numbers more than double when we focus on Millennials. How do you appeal to people who embrace these strange fictions?

Figure 1. Percent who agree, are unsure, or disagree with three conspiracy claims, and with a basic scientific fact

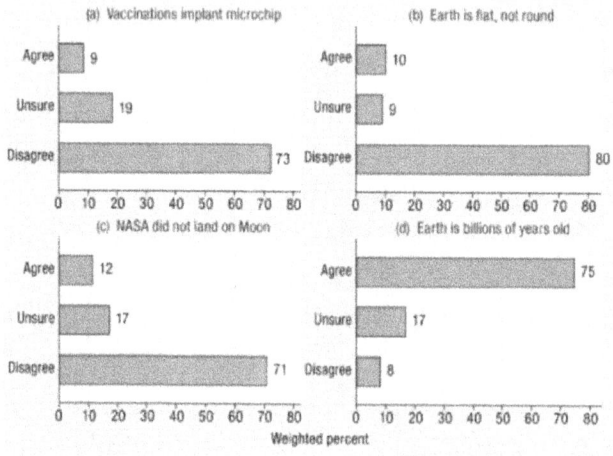

Figure 2. Percent who agree with nine conspiracy or scientific statements

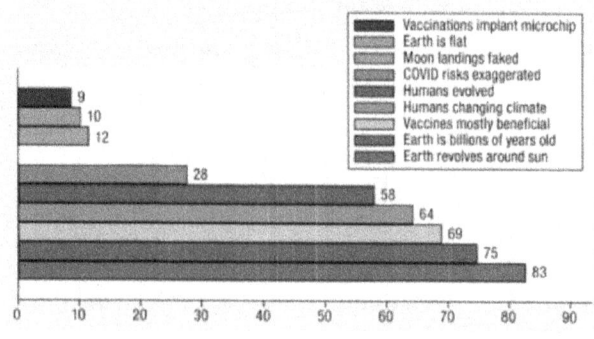

Source: POLES 2021 survey

Figure 4. Responses to four conspiracy or science statements, by generation of respondent

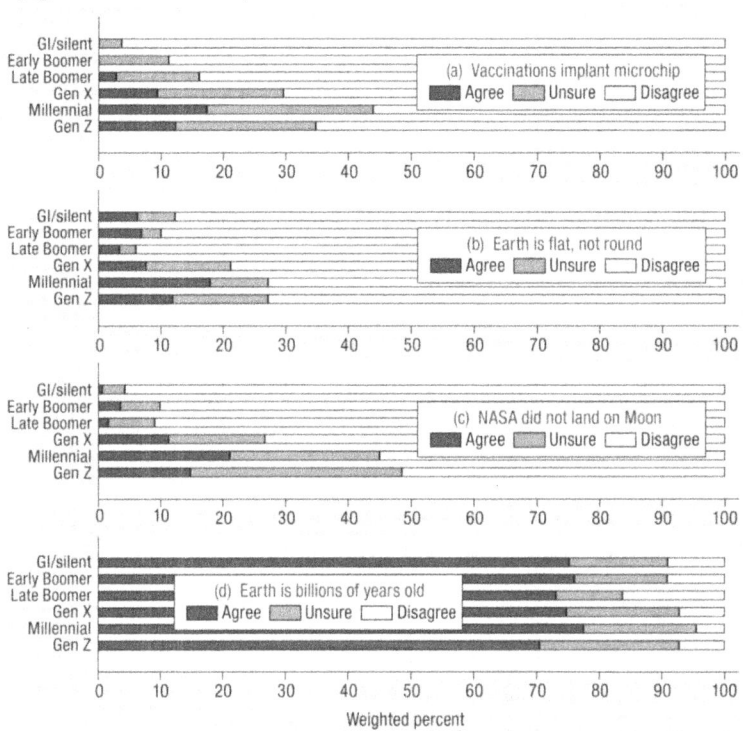

Note: Generational differences regarding vaccination microchips, flat Earth, and Moon landings are statistically significant (all p < 0.001); generational differences regarding age of the Earth are not significant (p = 0.77; all tests by ordered logit regression). **Source:** *POLES 2021 survey.*

It might be easy to dismiss those people as uneducated or gullible, but they have healthcare needs, too. They need to be engaged, and we need to communicate with them. Our mission compels us to meet people where they are, even when they believe things we are adamantly against or know to be untrue.

Today's era is being characterized as the "Experience Age," in a shift from the "Information Age."

The Experience Age is a term used to describe the transition from the Information Age to a new era where digital interactions are focused on experiences rather than just data consumption. This concept is driven by immersive technologies, real-time engagement, and the shift from passive content consumption to interactive and participatory experiences. The delivery of truth is shifting.

I'm not suggesting that authentic marketing acknowledges that the world might be flat. It just means that we must find ways to communicate in a way they can understand and appreciate. It means we can acknowledge that some people believe the world is flat without attacking them or talking down to them for their beliefs.

Above all, it means delivering an accurate and truthful message in a way that will resonate with everyone, regardless of the "tribe" they've chosen and the echo chamber they live in.

Data, analytics, and consumer research introduces the science into marketing. It starts with learning about our audiences to predict what messages and messengers are going to resonate with which audience. Those audiences have preferences in the ways that they engage and receive information and are key to our connection with them. Lastly, the right data and analytics tools monitoring the success of our predictions allow us to make ongoing adjustments as we continually learn.

The bottom line is that as a marketer, I have to acknowledge that there are things people believe that I don't agree with. We don't have to say we agree with them, but we need to show empathy for how they feel in order to reach them.

USING THE RIGHT TOOLS

With all that said, let's dive into the question of what type of analytics, data, and research healthcare marketers should use. I won't dive deeply into the details here; my purpose here is to offer a way to think about marketing, and I don't want to waste your time in the weeds.

A great foundation for approaching this subject is to acknowledge that there are first-party and second-party sources of data you can use in analytics. The combination of these provides the balance of factual and emotional details to help us craft our marketing strategies and content.

An example of first-party data is the very data that hospitals create themselves. They know the patients they have treated and a great deal about them. You can take that data and see what insurance they have, where they live, how old they are, what procedures they've had and when, and numerous other data points—then cross-reference that with marketing outreach efforts and second-party data sources.

What else can you uncover about them? Income and other financial info, like charitable giving? Other types of purchases and brands they prefer? Education? Do they follow their physicians' advice? Take their medications? Eat well? Are they registered to vote, and if so, are they are registered as a Democrat, Republican, or Independent? Do they vote regularly?

You can collect all kinds of data from different platforms and information sources to give you a much clearer picture of a single individual, from which you can create an Ideal Customer Profile (ICP) across all service lines.

Then there are research tools you can deploy both online and via more traditional means, like phone surveys. Let me give you a quick but detailed example.

In a typical public opinion polling, let's say I have five messages I want to test. One of the messages tests at 72 percent effective, while another is 68 percent, and another 59 percent. But that's not the most interesting data because it's all aggregated.

No, the most interesting data is when you dig into it to find the spikes in efficacy. For example, the first message might test at 72 percent overall, but with self-identified MAGA Republicans, it tests at 87 percent. Now you know that message will be more effective with that group. That same message might test at 31 percent with Democrats and 50 percent with Independents.

First, you have to actually care to ask that question. And second, you have to develop messages to test. This means you have to create messages that are still authentic but can be received in this post-truth world. The testing should go way beyond political affiliation and look at many other factors.

You can make use of data to create profiles so that you can more accurately understand who your target audience is. Then you can conduct research to ensure that what you *believe* you need to say is what you *actually need to say* in order to reach the person.

There are far too many tools, sources, and approaches to discuss in detail here. I do want you to understand that there are different types of analytics and tools available to help you reach the right people with the right message.

BALANCING FACTS AND EMOTION

Earlier in the book, I touched on the concept that good marketing should appeal to both the head and the heart. As we talk about data-driven marketing in this chapter, perhaps this is good time to look at how we balance it with emotions and storytelling.

Part of being authentic is to understand our audiences at a deeper level, even being able to understand emotions that our audiences may not be aware of or be able to articulate. There are research techniques and methods that enable us to really get beneath the surface, including beyond the spoken word.

Data analytics is able to do that by analyses that can look at a variety of influencing factors, including drivers. But sensitive and purposeful qualitative research can look in a different way. How do people feel about having early-onset Alzheimer's? What does having terminal cancer feel like? How does it feel to deal with that level of fear? What about giving birth, or the inner emotional strains of being a caregiver? Do people behind the research really understand how it feels? You get the picture.

Getting to a deeper understanding of these feelings by spending time exploring them is as important as data analytics. It may not be a fashionable view, but it is based in the search for authenticity. Healthcare is a human experience, and often an incredibly powerful one. The best creative work touches people in profound ways, and we need a deep understanding of people to do that.

Here's an example. If marketing is fact-driven, it will emphasize something like this: "We provide this many dollars in charity care, we provide these certain community benefits, we pay this much in taxes, we won these awards, we're in the top 100 of our industry," and so on. This is all designed to communicate facts, which are supposed to inspire confidence. And that approach will work—with some audiences.

On the other hand, if marketing is geared toward emotions, it will communicate something like this: "We care about you. We're here for you. We're mission driven." And that will work with other audiences.

In contrast to fact-driven marketing, emotion-driven marketing is designed to make you feel the institution or brand cares about you personally. They want you to feel loved.

It's rare to see these two approaches combined. For example, "We know you live a busy life and we care about you. We have created a very easy way of scheduling your appointments online to reduce friction for you. We have a 24/7 call center that isn't just open when you're at work, but all the time. We are providing this tool so you know what you have to pay for before you receive care."

That's an imaginary example, of course, because few healthcare systems in America do all three of those things equally well. But that's an example of how to include both an emotional and a factual appeal in the same marketing message—i.e., we care about you, we are mission-driven, and we are backing that up with specific factual elements. We want your life to be easier and we have taken steps to make that happen.

My clients sometimes ask me whether they should be putting money into building their brand or performance marketing to help them acquire customers.

My answer is always *yes*.

I don't see an inherent tradeoff between those two things. Brand-building is generally seen as an emotional exercise, while acquiring patients is seen as a factual exercise. But I don't look at them as distinctly different. They should always be interrelated. They should work symbiotically by leveraging the brand to acquire patients, and also acquiring and retaining patients in a way that builds the brand.

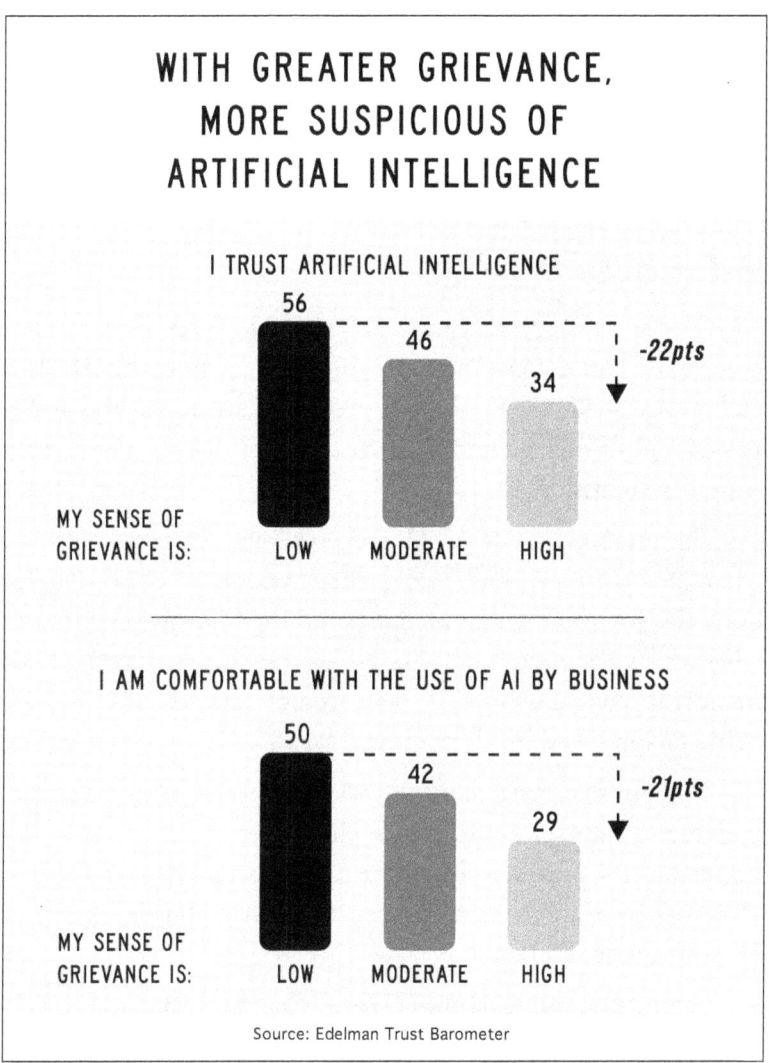

WITH GREATER GRIEVANCE, MORE SUSPICIOUS OF ARTIFICIAL INTELLIGENCE

I TRUST ARTIFICIAL INTELLIGENCE

56   46   34   -22pts

MY SENSE OF
GRIEVANCE IS: LOW   MODERATE   HIGH

I AM COMFORTABLE WITH THE USE OF AI BY BUSINESS

50   42   29   -21pts

MY SENSE OF
GRIEVANCE IS: LOW   MODERATE   HIGH

Source: Edelman Trust Barometer

The data backs this up and moves the modern marketer past the *theory* that a strong brand and effective performance marketing are interrelated and puts that concept into daily decision-making practice.

In our research, there is a correlation between composite brand strength (usually preference and/or trust) and campaign cost per lead (our most common key performance indicator [KPI] for patient acquisition). As brand strength increases, cost per lead decreases until you reach a tipping point. More on that later.

WHERE DOES AI FIT IN?

Any discussion of analytics, research, and data in the context of authenticity needs to include the topic of AI. This technological force has become so ubiquitous in culture, and is progressing at such a rapid pace, that we have consider how it fits into this discussion.

The mere existence of AI makes people mistrust much of what they see, hear, and read. When you query ChatGPT, for example, you don't know where it's pulling information from or whether it's accurate. People almost assume that AI is going to be inauthentic on some level. People are not sure whether they are being manipulated, so they assume the worst in many cases.

Therefore, we have to assume that the use of AI in marketing is going to raise all kinds of new challenges. There are also new opportunities, of course, but those come with perhaps the biggest challenge for marketers, which is ensuring that AI does not impair or compromise authenticity.

Should you use AI? I think, *yes*. It's a remarkable tool to help you be more efficient and effective, which therefore has all kinds of positive cascading effects. But again, we have to make sure we are doing it in a manner that is transparent and authentic.

For example, there is a radio station in my area that runs a promo along these lines (I'm paraphrasing): "We use AI to generate certain commercials and promotions. We want you to feel confident that we would never use AI in a way that is

How Cigna Saves Millions by Having Its Doctors Reject Claims Without Reading Them

When a stubborn pain in Nick van Terheyden's bones would not subside, his doctor had a hunch what was wrong.

Without enough vitamin D in the blood, the body will pull calcium from the bones. Left untreated, a vitamin D deficiency can lead to osteoporosis.

If we want to do the same thing in healthcare, we can tell our audience that we know they are concerned about the use of AI. We will share how we will use it, and how we won't. That is one simple way to use AI ethically and authentically to build trust instead of eroding it.

Now let me give you the flip side—what I would see as an inauthentic use of AI. All the big health insurance companies use AI to review claims so they can decide when to deny a claim or a pre-authorization.

In a surprise to no one, all those health insurance companies have tuned their AI to over-index on denials in the extreme. For example, it was reported that in a single two-month period, doctors working for Cigna denied over 300,000 requests for payment using this "method" (as they refer to it). The average review time for each case was 1.2 seconds.[12]

---

12 Patrick Rucker, Maya Miller, and David Armstrong, "How Cigna Saves Millions by Having Its Doctors Reject Claims Without Reading Them," *ProPublica*, March 25, 2023, https://www.propublica.org/article/cigna-pxdx-medical-health-insurance-rejection-claims.

By the same token, UnitedHealth Group was the subject of a class-action lawsuit by some of its members who were denied coverage. According to an article in *Healthcare Finance*, "They claim in the lawsuit that the use of AI to evaluate claims for post-acute care resulted in denials, which in turn led to worsening health for the patients and in some cases resulted in death. They said the AI program developed by UnitedHealth subsidiary naviHealth, nH Predict, would sometimes supersede physician judgement, and has a 90% error rate, meaning nine of 10 appealed denials were ultimately reversed."[13]

Those are the most inauthentic uses of AI that I can possibly imagine. It is not being used to identify problems (and solutions). It is being deployed to actively harm people and to deny payment for their care—care that people know they might not receive if it gets denied. Cigna's advertising states it cares about people, and yet its AI deployment around claims denials proves the exact opposite.

Cigna's customers, like all health plan consumers, are paying premiums to cover their healthcare costs, and then the company uses AI in a way that is completely working against their own stated mission.

This behavior is also a great example of inauthentic marketing because their marketing is tuned to appeal to emotions, while their delivery (i.e., what they actually provide) is mis-tuned factually. This kind of abuse of trust, played out over their entire customer base, can have devastating consequences for a company's bottom line.

In this chapter, I have shared a few big-picture principles for using analytics, data, and research in our healthcare marketing.

---

13 Jeff Lagasse, "Class Action Lawsuit Against UnitedHealth's AI Claim Denials Advances," *Healthcare Finance News*, February 4, 2025, https://www.healthcarefinancenews.com/news/class-action-lawsuit-against-unitedhealths-ai-claim-denials-advances

I haven't attempted to give you a detailed playbook because that will be different depending on your specific organization, mission, supporting marketing efforts, and the various other nuanced factors in your situation. My goal here is not to tell you what to do. It's to help you understand how you think about what you do.

In Chapter Four, we will build on what we have learned so far and explore how to think about your marketing plan design.

CHAPTER FOUR

MILE MARKER #2—
PLAN DESIGN

Now that we have laid a foundation for the value of analytics, data, and research when developing healthcare marketing in a post-truth world, it's time to think about how to package that knowledge.

You're a marketer, and I understand the pressure you're under to deliver results. You always have a smaller budget than you think you need, the people above you want results yesterday, and then there is the pressure you put on yourself to perform.

As you've been reading this book, you're probably dancing between two lines of thought. You may be excited to read a different perspective on healthcare marketing. Yet you're also wondering what this new approach will cost you in terms of time, money, and energy. Sometimes it just feels easier to fall back on the familiar and proven rather than push forward with new approaches.

I urge you to keep an open mind as we continue to go through these mile markers. The only way to have meaningful change is to keep an open mind and be willing to try new things.

After all, if you treat audiences today like you've always treated them, you will continue to get the same results you've always gotten. Or more accurately, you will get diminishing results year after year, as times are rapidly changing.

With that in mind, let's begin by considering how marketing in our industry has changed in recent years. That will give us a solid foundation for thinking about how to design a new plan.

HOW HEALTHCARE MARKETING HAS CHANGED

In the first place, we have to admit that marketing in healthcare tends to trail other, more progressive industries by five to ten years. Email has been in use in the retail and travel industries since the late 1990s. CRM and targeted email marketing followed closely behind that. Online pricing and purchasing were available in the 2000s. That gap has narrowed some in the last few years, but we still have a long way to go.

Historically, healthcare marketers were brand marketers or communications professionals, not service line marketers. For that reason, you would find a lot of marketers who were adept at building brands through traditional advertising and driving name awareness, brand awareness, and even brand preference. Impressions, reach, and frequency of exposure were the goals.

That's a much different focus from actually getting someone to make a decision to use your service. And even brand building requires a new authentic marketing approach to be effective in the post-truth era.

In any given year, about one percent of the population accesses services at a hospital. In most markets, if you asked people to tell you if they recognize the name of this hospital or that hospital, the brand recognition is exceptional because hospitals have brand ID at 99 percent. Brand preference will measure differently for each organization, but it's not as if people don't know what hospitals are in their communities. They may not know much about them, and they may not know why they should choose one over another. However, they have some sense of these organizations from brand advertising.

The problem is, the impact of that brand advertising can be eroded by the latest negative news article, a public lawsuit about a patient outcome that was less than ideal, or another factor beyond your control.

Over the last few years in particular, we have seen a real acceleration in data-driven marketing for targeted service lines. In other words, the focus is on patient acquisition and retention. It has moved from *I want you to know my name and think nice things about me* to *I want you to know my name and think nice things about me, and I want you to choose me for X, Y, and Z services.*

The marketing message is that for X, Y, and Z, we are better than everyone else, or we are more accessible, or more available, or offer some other advantage. Data-driven marketing has facilitated the transition from big brand broadcast campaigns to much more targeted campaigns toward specific subgroups of people who are more likely to benefit from and choose certain services.

This is all a way of saying that healthcare marketing has become far more quantitatively driven than it used to be. It's much more targeted these days; yet there are all kinds of factors that prevent it from being as effective as it could be.

For example, I can't tell you the number of organizations that want to hire us to market certain service lines with long waiting lists. If you want us to market your GI services but your waiting list is six months long because you don't have enough doctors to open up more slots, there are certain strategies that make sense. However, it's likely a different mix than we would use for a service line, with a more open schedule and readily available appointment slots.

Remember those analytic capabilities we talked about in Mile Marker #1? Tying together the market demand, our service preference, capacity, and profitability might help us avoid this situation and keep us from deploying the tight marketing strategies for this constrained GI offering. Instead, we might focus on a similarly needed and valuable service where we do have capacity and brand familiarity. Or perhaps we even prioritize GI physician recruitment before resuming marketing efforts for that service offering.

Occasionally you're met with the reality that a certain physician is politically important. The CEO wants to keep them happy. There's an old joke in the industry that billboards don't work at all, but if you want to keep the doctors happy, just buy a billboard they will see on their drive home. Marketing that we can see is often viewed as more important or valuable than the powerful (but hidden) digital strategies that are carefully targeted to specific audiences.

That is perhaps an extreme example, and overall, healthcare marketing has become much more strategic, a value driver rather than a cost center. However, I will remind you that we are human, and humans are complex, with multiple incentives and motivators. The most significant shift has been from exclusively large, brand campaigns that are hard to track and measure in terms of business impact to more digital campaigns that are easier to manage and track in terms of ROI.

John Wannamaker famously said, "Half the money I spend on advertising is wasted; the trouble is I don't know which half." Increasingly, the perception is the brand portion.

That said, there is still a problem: Most healthcare organizations are measuring the effectiveness of what they're doing, but they're not necessarily recognizing what they're missing. They are not thinking about who they are not targeting and therefore not reaching.

So how exactly *do* you reach those skeptics? Let's explore a few thoughts.

REACHING SKEPTICS

One thing to keep in mind is that some groups embracing the post-truth era are not necessarily skeptical or hostile toward you specifically, but toward institutions and experts in general.

Let's assume, for the sake of argument, that we are reaching the middle of the political spectrum and the "center" of society reasonably well, or that we are reaching those people who are probably more motivated by facts and tend to view institutions and experts as more credible.

The focus, then, becomes doing a better job reaching those audiences that don't statistically fall into those two categories. That would be people who have a particular political leaning, particularly Millennials and younger people.

Younger people are much more likely to get their news solely from social media. They are also more likely to rely on the wisdom of the crowd, if you will, as opposed to facts and experts. In addition, they have some of the lowest trust numbers in institutions and experts overall. These are the people who will be healthcare's primary consumers in fifteen to twenty years. We will all be influencers in our parents' healthcare decisions now and in the future.

To be fair, they have come by it honestly. A good deal of our marketing is actually designed for the C-suite and the board that approved it, as opposed to the people who consume it.

I hear this complaint from lots of people. "We are running digital campaigns, but my board isn't targeted by those, so they don't think we're doing anything." That misses the point, of course, but it's also human nature. If you don't see it, you assume it's not happening.

But very often that is exactly why that marketing is effective. Naturally, that sixty-five-year-old male board member is not seeing the ad targeting childbearing-age women. The seventy-year-old female board member is not seeing marketing for prostate cancer care.

A few years ago, the CEO of one of my clients said to me, "I don't believe in digital. I believe in billboards and direct mail." But if you don't believe in digital, it's like saying you don't believe in air or sunshine. I don't even know how to respond to this reasoning. He may not like to consume information digitally, but it's absolutely how many others do. Ignoring it means ignoring effectiveness and impact, which we do at our own peril.

In the next chapter, we will dig into what it means to get your message and messenger correct. But for now, I want to emphasize that you must be saying the right things, hopefully with a blend of emotion and facts, and saying it through the right channels.

Is the message being delivered by someone your target audience is more likely to trust? Increasingly, it is not going to be experts, but a channel they trust with a messenger they identify with and find credible that effectively reaches a certain target demographic for you.

We know there are very few people who watch both MSNBC and Fox News. It tends to be one or the other or neither. We know there is a huge cohort that gets unreliable information from social media and from other online sources, but that doesn't mean we cannot participate in those channels in an authentic way.

BUILDING FLEXIBILITY INTO YOUR PLAN

As you develop an overall strategy and marketing plan, keep in mind that it is not a "set it and forget it" type of thing. You need flexibility to adapt because things can change quickly.

The solution is to build in flexibility for all the realities. In other words, you are not just planning for failure. You're planning for success. For example, if you are running a GI or heart campaign, how will you know that it's working well enough that you can shift strategies on that service offering? If your plan is successful, then at some point the schedule will be full, and there will be a waiting list. Once that happens, you don't have to keep marketing going at the same intensity, but rather can pull back in the right way at the right time.

At what point are you collaborating with business development, physician recruitment, and operations about who needs to be hired next? Is it a male or female physician, physician's assistant, or other type of provider?

If you continue the same approach with the same group, it will actually backfire because you will have far more patients who need that service than you can handle. I know that "planning for success" is not something healthcare marketers often consider, but it's vital to monitor if you want a robust marketing campaign to yield maximum results for the lowest overall cost.

You should constantly be measuring your effectiveness and impact, then adjust the plan for what you are learning. If you are overperforming, pull back a little bit. If you are underperforming, you'll need to adjust one or more of your variables (target market, messaging, etc.) or allocate more resources.

We are seeing this in politics now, where big super PACs will not run ads that have not been tested within an inch of their lives. They are spending around ten times as much on creative campaigns because they are developing essentially ten campaigns, testing all of them, and then running one or two that show the greatest efficacy. This approach is particularly important with niche audiences most affected by the post-truth era.

For example, an article in *The New York Times* noted the influence of Future Forward, an especially powerful super PAC, during the 2024 election cycle:

> The group is, in some ways, an ad-making laboratory masquerading as a super PAC, testing thousands of messages, social media posts and ads in the 2024 race, ranking them in order of effectiveness and approving only those that resonate with voters. Ad makers produce roughly 20 potential commercials for every spot that ever airs. And Future Forward has conducted nearly four million voter surveys since Ms. Harris entered the race—and more than 10 million since January.[14]

---

14 Theodore Schleifer and Shane Goldmacher, "Future Forward, Backing Kamala Harris, Is Now the Biggest Spender in the 2024 Race," *The New York Times*, October 17, 2024, https://www.nytimes.com/2024/10/17/us/elections/future-forward-kamala-harris-ads.html

The tail used to wag the dog. You never tested creative, and the advertising agencies made all their money buying media. Just watch an episode of *Mad Men*.

That is not so much the case anymore. The creative serves the critical function of getting people's attention, getting them to engage. You can test that and constantly optimize creative for different audiences.

Everyone talks about personalized marketing, but it's not as easy as snapping your fingers. First of all, in order to be personalized, it has to be authentic. It must connect with people on a human level and on an individual level based on their demographics, socioeconomics, and psychographics.

And second, it has to acknowledge the post-truth era. There are various cohorts of the population, and your marketing campaigns will have to look, feel, and sound different to each of those audiences you want to reach.

In the next chapter, we will build on what we have discussed about analytics and plan design as we consider how to give hands and feet to your marketing via your message and the messenger.

CHAPTER FIVE

MILE MARKER #3– THE MESSAGE AND MESSENGER

The next mile marker on our journey flows directly from the first two. Once you have identified authentic insights and created a strategic springboard, or plan, it's time to focus on the message, the messenger, and the audience.

We know many audiences will reject the "doctor in a white lab coat" image in the post-truth era. With that in mind, what do credibility and authority look like in a post-truth environment? Are you tapping into those different credible sources, including influencers you might be missing, since much of your audience is listening to them in this post-truth era?

As a marketer, you will need to lean into sources, influencers, and channels you may not be comfortable with in order to reach people. In this chapter, I want to help you get more comfortable with doing just that.

Begin by asking, *What is the message saying?* and *Who is saying it?* Once you nail down those elements, you will move on to the channels where you will disseminate the message. (That's the topic of the next chapter.)

People are much more likely to engage with someone who seems like them, who believes what they believe, and who delivers messages that they haven't already decided they disagree with.

WHAT MAKES A MESSAGE RESONATE?

With any marketing message, particularly in healthcare, simpler is better.

If a message fits on a bumper sticker, it will probably be remembered more than a LinkedIn post. If it's a LinkedIn post, it will be remembered more than a three-page document. If it's a three-page document, it will be remembered more than a book. (Well, maybe not this book, but you get the point.)

That's simply the reality of our post-truth era. But it's also a product of our post-reading economy.

People don't consume volumes of written information the way they used to. We crave simplicity and brevity these days. In my view, a great deal of healthcare marketing is either factual or emotional, but rarely both. That's why the best messages are framed and delivered in a way that blends facts and emotion.

There's an old quote from Theodore Roosevelt: "People don't care how much you know until they know how much you care." That's especially true in the healthcare sector. People will not trust what we're saying unless they know we care about something other than ourselves.

However, there's an emotional angle to that. Simple brevity, plus a combination of facts and emotions, equals what I call fact-based empathy. The big gap here is that healthcare providers very rarely use humor.

Right now, you may be thinking, *Humor? In healthcare? That feels tone deaf.* Yet humor is a powerful way of defusing opposition and anger, and properly deployed it connects directly to people's hearts. Humor also demonstrates that we don't take ourselves too seriously, even on serious subjects.

One of the most memorable ads in our space was run by UnitedHealthcare a few years ago. It showed people having weird accidents, then the screen would flash with a billing code for the accident. It was very clever and funny because they used lots of strange words and phrased to code what happened to people. UHC was basically making fun of the system.

These days, UnitedHealthcare is not a funny subject. However, we can recognize good marketing from any company, no matter how much we disapprove of their business practices.

Providers don't take this approach very often because we associate emotion with being sappy and humor with tone deafness. Think about the crying mother holding a newborn, or the person sitting by a bed, holding someone's hand as they are dying. Those kinds of ads have their place, but they're overused. We can tell a highly empathetic story about a serious topic yet still bring a little humor into it.

Most advertising tends to be focused on the head or the heart. It rarely speaks to both. The best marketing accesses both its intended audience's emotions and need for factual information.

To be blunt, a huge part of the healthcare marketing space is just boring. It's because so much of our "news" and information is really just entertainment and opinion pieces that are repackaged. Our industry's safe, middle-of-the-road creativity and messaging lacks tailoring to specific audiences struggles to break through the clutter and will continue to do so—unless we change course.

Linda MacCracken[15] is a professor at Harvard, a former Associate Director of Consumer Engagement at Accenture, and served as Vice President at Truven and Thomson Reuters. She noted, "Break-thru messaging depends on the most effective Who (are the target customer types), Where (are they in the search and selection process), What (is the job they want done by the provider they pick for the health challenge), and How (will we tell the story) … The chance to stand out in being accessible ahead of shifting insurer networks moves the provider to the head of the line."

People in healthcare organizations feel strongly about facts and science and about being honest and direct. It is easy to stop taking risks and avoid doing new and interesting things. Although I believe we can be both fact-based as well as creative in our marketing, there are notable reasons why healthcare has usually avoiding doing anything risky. Let's explore why.

WHY HEALTHCARE MARKETING AVOIDS RISK

Other industries are much more likely to take chances, and that's appropriate. Consider the sports, movie, and music industries. If they screw up something, it's not the end of the world.

Yet if a health system makes an error that goes public, it has very real consequences for people's health and their very lives. However, that's not the only factor creating a situation where marketers in hospitals and health systems—and the whole healthcare provider industry in general—tend to avoid risk. Remember all of those tests a physician orders regardless of the patient's ability to pay for them?

---

15 MacCracken, Linda. Document sent to the author. March 8, 2025.

The involvement of health insurance, and the reality that people receiving the service are generally not the ones paying the majority of the bill, creates a complex system where no single entity seems responsible for the outcome.

We also have a dynamic in healthcare where many people don't think of patients as consumers. I have clients who refuse to use that word. They only talk about patients. It misses a huge opportunity to recognize that we need to provide an experience to consumers that is as good as they would receive from a large consumer brand.

The irony is that every single consumer will one day be a patient. But patients at hospitals and health systems represent only 1 percent of the population in any given year.

If I had to pinpoint one single thing as the reason why we avoid risk, it's the attitude of "Let's not screw this up," as opposed to "Let's try some new things we haven't done before."

I promise you, no hospital CEO has ever uttered the phrase "Let's fail fast and break things." That's partly because these are very large institutions that have been around for a long time. It's easy to get bound to a certain culture and decision-making process. It's easy to rely on yesterday's marketing strategy rather than trying new things and reaching people in new ways.

In healthcare, we also battle the belief that it's extremely hard to do new, interesting things when you are starved for resources. When your budget is lean, you're not going to try a new, risky approach. You will focus on initiatives and approaches that have the highest possible chance of success. That probably means something you have done before, likely *many* times before. In other cases, when budgets are tight, CFOs often want to slash marketing spend when it's the very thing the organization needs to bring new patients into their health system.

Yet another factor that makes it hard to take risks is the amount of regulatory overlay, such as privacy concerns and restrictions on marketing, that is unique to healthcare. What is perfectly normal in other industries is often illegal in healthcare.

For marketers, it is easy to feel beaten down over time. You develop a defeatist attitude, thinking, *The C-suite will just say no anyway*, or *We can't afford to think outside the box.*

Healthcare culture is built upon science-based principles—clinical trials, evidence, and proven treatments, just to name a few. That culture permeates the whole industry. That isn't necessarily a bad thing. However, a high-quality marketing culture needs to have an element of "let's try this" or "let's take a calculated risk." This calculated risk lets us try something that hasn't been done before, and the predominant healthcare culture needs to accept that.

That said, in the end, the winners will separate themselves from the rest because they are willing to go beyond their comfort zone, try new things, and reach the people in their target audience in ways that authentically resonate.

THE DOCTOR IN A WHITE LAB COAT

Let's close this chapter by zooming out a bit and examining one of the most ubiquitous images in all healthcare marketing: the doctor in a white lab coat. That single image represents so much of what is not working: a reliance on experts and institutions.

Public cynicism about medical professionals is so high that Cigna created a spoof video titled "TV Doctors of America."v The hilarious ad features TV doctors such as Alan Alda (from *M*A*S*H*) and Noah Wyle (from *ER* and *The Pitt*) encouraging people to get their annual physical.

Why have TV doctors become the butt of the joke over time? What are the reasons most people are suspicious of the supposed experts in white lab coats? There are four primary ones.

1. THE UBIQUITOUS AVAILABILITY OF UNVETTED INFORMATION.

The accessibility of information on the internet has made everyone feel like an expert, even when they are not. You don't see people just going in to see their doctor—they are coming in with sheets of paper printed with information from WebMD because they have already self-diagnosed.

People's minds always jump to the worst conclusions. They assume they have contracted an obscure sub-Saharan Africa virus. No one ever says, "I'm pretty sure I have a common cold." It's much more common for them to assume they have something serious.

The information they have used to self-diagnose may not always be accurate. It may not have been vetted. But it does mean they are choosing to trust it instead of a trained doctor.

2. THE RELATIVE DIFFICULTY OF ACCESSING, AND GETTING INFORMATION FROM, YOUR DOCTOR.

A multitude of barriers have been created to make it harder for you to get complete information from a doctor—and to simply get in to see them in the first place.

It's difficult to get a timely appointment. And when you do show up for the meeting you scheduled months in advance, the staff sits with their back to you, typing EHR information into a computer. That behavior compromises a sense of personal connection and trust.

Yet it's not really the doctor's fault. They are simply one cog in a much larger system mostly controlled by insurance companies.

The insurance company requires more and more data; the government asks for documentation; and thus the health system that employs the physician built an office around the paperwork and not the patient.

When your doctor orders a lab or procedure, and the insurance company refuses it, you question to some degree whether the doctor was wrong or if the lab or procedure was necessary to begin with. The system seems almost designed to undermine your trust in it. It begs the question of whom you should trust: the insurance company, the doctor, or perhaps no one?

3. THE COLLECTIVE RECOGNITION THAT EXPERTS HAVE OFTEN BEEN WRONG.

This started before COVID, but the pandemic only accelerated the latent mistrust of medical experts. Over the last few years, much information has come out about misguided decisions during COVID, and it has created a real inflection point in our attitude toward experts.

The consequences of being wrong were so big that it's impossible to ignore the massive sense of mistrust. The world doesn't need another person to pick on Dr. Fauci, but some of his admissions that we knew certain things were wrong—but they said and did them anyway—have contributed to the current post-truth environment.

This whole experience violated our collective notion that scientists are supposed to be objective and avoid a political agenda.

4. THE CONSTANT PITCHING OF PRODUCTS BY "DOCTORS" ON ALL SORTS OF MEDIA.

Can we agree that this has been overdone to the point where it's not just ineffective, but is working against our trust in healthcare?

You have a doctor pitching you on using Icy Hot, and another pitching you on using an all-body deodorant, then another talking to you about getting hearing screenings or cancer care.

The appearance of doctors in advertising has become so normalized that it doesn't mean anything anymore. Half the time, you're not even sure it's a real doctor—which has given birth to the common joke, "I'm not a doctor, and I don't play one on TV."

WE CAN DO BETTER

Taken together, the four reasons I just shared have created an environment in our post-truth era where we have an element of mistrust, and sometimes even outright hostility, baked into the way we see doctors and healthcare institutions.

It's why the principles we have talked about in this chapter are so key. People have to trust the message and the messenger. And it probably won't entail picturing a doctor in a white lab coat.

We can do better—*much* better. But rather than seeing our post-truth era as a huge challenge or obstacle, what if we see it as an opportunity to serve people more deeply and to become our best selves as individuals and institutions?

Larry Weber writes in *Authentic Marketing*:

> In this era, I believe marketing will become its best self—a more transparent, more genuine, more interesting, and less manipulative discipline. Companies must behave with more humanity, listening and responding to customers and operating every day with their values in mind. As their moral purpose comes to life, they should be sharing genuine, compelling stories about

> the ways they are working to positively
> impact people and the planet. Finally,
> companies should ensure their products do
> more harm than good.[16]

Similar to the Hippocratic Oath physicians take when they enter their profession, the central tenet of "doing no harm" has created our basic viewpoint on the medical field: It should do more good than harm. Ideally, it should do no harm at all.

It is time for healthcare marketers to adopt the same viewpoint. While we use many tools, like data, analytics, and AI to learn and craft strategies, it is all for the greater purpose of doing good for people.

In the next chapter, we will explore how to take what you have learned so far and apply it to appropriate marketing channels to ensure your message—and messenger—get the attention they deserve.

Healthcare advertising is overwhelmingly inauthentic. There are so many campaigns that all look the same, depicting happy people (presumably ex-patients) being happy, doing happy things in happy places. They all look so healthy and joyful. It is the ultimate sugar coating and is anything but authentic.

Healthcare advertising and marketing communication should be some of the best in the world—the most emotional, the most creative, the most poignant. The category can literally be about life or death. The setting is a place where the most intense drama can occur. It's a sector with drama built in. It's no surprise that TV dramas revisit the hospital setting time and time again.

I think it is safe to say that all of us, at some time or another, have had a health worry or know someone really well who has.

---

16 Weber, *Authentic* Marketing, 73.

Even the smallest concern can play tricks on our mind and set us off on some irrational course of action, and the most serious conditions will be some of the most challenging times in our lives—as a patient or a caregiver or just as an emotionally involved party.

Everyone knows that healthcare advertising is not really how people experience healthcare. It's an upbeat approximation. Why can't we be more authentic? People know what it is really like. Don't disrespect them with the sugar coating. People can accept the reality of healthcare. Let's be real.

Consider the story of a mother's increasingly loud and desperate screams of "Oh my God, oh my God!" as she realizes it's her son who is lying beside a serious motorbike crash. As she runs toward the crash scene, her phone remains on and it captures everything she says in her moments of anguish.

Or consider the Macmillan Cancer Support film *Whatever It Takes*, a Cannes Lion Winner in 2021. It showed the tears, the tragedy, the fears, the joy, the hope, and the pain of cancer, with no holds barred.

Finally, consider the story of a road trip for a father and son traveling together to the Mayo Clinic, where the son is going for cancer care.

We don't need to sugarcoat the truth. People can handle the realities of life—which at some point involves heartbreak and death for everyone. These three breathtakingly beautiful and absolutely authentic pieces are just a few examples.

But our messaging can't end there. It's not enough to just understand or accept people's pain and suffering. We have to reach them where they are. That's where going to the people we serve via the right marketing channels comes in. We'll explore this topic in the next chapter.

CHAPTER SIX

MILE MARKER #4– MARKETING CHANNELS

For some readers, a chapter on marketing channels may feel like the most important part of the book. After all, at the end of the day, the core question you're concerned with is, "How do I reach the most consumers in order to provide the support they need and create the most value possible for my organization?"

As I mentioned earlier in the book, my aim isn't to give a detailed guide on how, what, and when to use certain channels to reach your goals. Every situation is different.

Even if it were possible to craft a guide like that, it would soon go out of date because specific channels, just like your organization's needs, are constantly changing.

The main point I want to make is this: If you show up with the usual messages, the usual messengers, and in the usual channels, that will ensure you will continue to miss a lot of people. And based on the rate of change we are experiencing, today's channels are likely to be irrelevant in five years.

We must adapt the channels we use in the post-truth era. That means a much more aggressive embrace and engagement in social media. In addition, it means aggressively engaging with people on particular social channels where you may not feel personally comfortable. Some of those people may not match your politics, whatever direction you lean.

I'm essentially arguing for a "pan-tribal" approach. This means you can't just market to the tribe you're comfortable with, or the one where you're a member. In short, the best practice is using all channels to reach all tribes, as much as possible.

CHANNELS AND CONSUMERS

This begs the question of how to know which channels to use to reach specific consumers. This is why the earlier chapter on analytics is so important. When you dig into the data and analytics, you can create ideal customer profiles (ICPs) for each service line, which is essential in marketing. Programmatic buying platforms have become much more sophisticated in reaching those ICPs across available digital media channels.

Some people focus on customer journey mapping, where you use data and analytics to identify what people need to hear, and where you need to meet them. It uses decision-making and media consumption patterns that examine the levels of trust in information they receive from different sources and at different stages in the decision-making journey. It also uses psychographics and other elements to give you as complete a picture of that consumer as possible.

This approach is often used by consumer-packaged goods (CPG) companies, which know the difference between, say, how detergent brands A, B, and C connect with consumers. Those companies have identified that certain words and images showing up in certain places are going to be more likely to engage their ideal customers. The same thing is true in healthcare.

Let me share a concept we're working on at Unlock Health.

We get asked all of the time how we would balance investments in brand advertising, earned media, digital paid media, and performance marketing in the health system marketing budget. It's the right question: How should a health system or other provider organization leverage paid/earned/owned to allocate marketing budget between brand building and performance marketing efforts?

The answer should not be informed by budget alone. The answer should be driven by data.

As you know, any healthcare brand can support many strategic priorities, including driving patient acquisition, building trust within their community, enhancing their regional or national reputation, and positioning the organization as an employer of choice. And there are multiple ways to improve your brand—not only via traditional media advertising but also through earned media, community engagement and sponsorships, and more.

In our research, there is a correlation between composite brand strength (usually preference and/or trust) and campaign cost per lead (our most common KPI for patient acquisition). We know this intuitively as marketers, but over the years we haven't been able to quantify this and use it to plan and operate more effectively.

But here's where things get interesting due to a tipping point. When a brand passes a certain strength threshold, campaign cost per lead decreases almost exponentially. The correlation between brand equity and effective cost per lead is *not* linear.

When we do this, a series of "next best actions" start to become possible. The next best action is the decision about what next offer or engagement to place in front of a consumer based on where they are in a journey.

This use is more about the follow-on prescriptive models that can be implemented to reflect our learnings as better decision-making with respect to budgets.

1. *Improved marketing mix modeling (MMM).* If we consider every patient acquisition campaign is also a brand campaign, and we know the status of our brand strength, we can be intentional about how much of our budget is invested in each of our paid, earned, and owned channels from the get-go.

2. *Measuring the impact of brand marketing, including earned media, on the bottom line.* By standardizing brand strength and patient acquisition KPIs over time, we develop a clear link between improvements in brand strength and improvements to the bottom line.

3. *Faster marketing diagnostics.* Using the tipping point, we can more quickly find ways optimize our campaign channels, messages, and calls to action. Removing the guesswork from growth means less time debating, more time executing, and faster speed to value.

Together, we can work toward the long-term goal of an aggregate brand equity KPI. Through advanced attribution modeling, we can differentiate between channels that are purely transactional and those that contribute to long-term patient loyalty, allowing for smarter budget allocation and campaign optimizations.

Finding the tipping point is the crux of a modern healthcare marketing strategy. Find it, and you're starting off new campaigns with the right channel mix and content and then optimizing more effectively. Launch without it, and you're stuck measuring the same old clicks, impressions, and views without ever tying your work back to bottom-line growth.

This connects to our conversation about marketing channels because, in our post-truth era, people don't know whom to trust. They distrust institutions and experts, so where do they go?

That is why we have to show up in the right places. We have to go to them instead of expecting them to come to us.

As Seth Godin writes in *All Marketers are Liars,*

```
    Don't try to change someone's worldview
is the strategy smart marketers follow.
Don't try to use facts to prove your case
and to insist that people change their
biases. You don't have time and you don't
have enough money. Instead, identify a
population with a certain worldview, frame
your story in terms of that worldview and
you win.[17]
```

I don't want to get too detailed when it comes to what specific social media channels offer, since it's constantly changing. That said, it's worthwhile to know a few basics.

Many people equate Facebook with "social media" because it has incredible brand recognition and has been around for a very long time (at least in relative terms of a social media company's life span). However, if you want to reach employers and business audiences, LinkedIn will be your best bet.

---

17 Seth Godin, *All Marketers Are Liars,* 41.

If you want to focus on partisan audiences, platforms such as Truth Social and Bluesky are the way to go. Many people and companies have returned to X (formerly Twitter) recently because it now caters more to a specific demographic than in the pre-Musk era.

In addition, if you're a large multinational corporation, you probably want a presence on X because its owner is very influential when it comes to how the federal government spends money. After DOGE launched, there was much written about Omnicom and IPG's return to X out of concern that refusing to do so might invite additional regulatory scrutiny of their proposed merger. We will never know if that would have happened.

I've been doing this long enough to remember when we used to refer to digital in healthcare organizations as "interactive." The common assumption was that seniors would never use it. Then at some point, everything changed, and seniors became the fastest-growing cohort on Facebook. Now Facebook is largely ignored by younger audiences in the U.S.

If you're a younger person today, you're not even going to Facebook. You'll use Instagram, TikTok, YouTube, or some other newer, smaller, niche platform.

This evolution has all happened primarily in the last ten or twelve years. As you're aware, these dynamics are always changing. Yet it's vital to be aware of the audiences for each platform and how they might expand your reach.

HOW CHANNELS HAVE CHANGED HEALTHCARE MARKETING

Speaking of constant change, let's take a few moments to think about how some of the more common channels have changed marketing for healthcare in recent years. Understanding the past can help us anticipate what the next few years may hold.

This may sound like a contradiction to much of what I've said in the book so far, but I don't believe social media has changed healthcare marketing as much as it should have.

One of the trends we've seen is a very significant shift away from spending the majority of an advertising budget on traditional advertising in TV to now focusing that spend on search engine marketing—Google in particular.

Hospitals and health systems are devoting substantially more of their resources to highly targeted digital media patient acquisition strategies via Google than ever before. It's especially accelerated in the post-COVID era. There has been a secular shift that accelerated after COVID but began well before that. This may have been further exacerbated by competing with providers outside your geography due to telehealth and other digital treatment protocols.

And of course everyone believes that AI tools such as ChatGPT and many others are going to have an increasing impact on every type of marketing, not just in healthcare. Everyone is watching how, over time, search traffic is impacted by AI as well.

Much of what we are talking about here is all about sharing information that helps people make better decisions, as opposed to choosing for them and then trying to get them to see our point of view. This is a very "top of the funnel" way of thinking, as opposed to just converting a lead.

Healthcare marketing has not kept up quite that well with most industries in terms of responding to this new era. We are doing a little better in moving dollars from traditional broadcast TV into cable, streaming, and other areas. Still, the focus remains on talking *at* people, not *with* people.

In general, we have done an inadequate job communicating in environments where you have to talk with people and engage them and their opinions. Case in point: If you are going to have a presence on Instagram, you need to engage with commenters and not just post videos or images. The same is true on LinkedIn, Facebook, YouTube, or any social media platform.

Healthcare marketers are not adjusting their ad spend mix enough because it feels risky and a little scary. They're not quite sure what to expect on those platforms, and they're concerned about what people may say in an uncontrolled environment.

Maybe they are biased about the audience. If you're more conservative, the last thing you probably want to do is communicate with a bunch of people on Bluesky. Likewise, if you're progressive, the last thing you probably want to do is engage on Truth Social.

I'm not suggesting this is all conscious bias. Many times, we don't pay attention to certain channels simply because they are not on our radar. Therefore, we don't prioritize them because they are not obvious to us. Recently, someone said to me, "I have never listened to a podcast in my life. I don't understand the value."

Since I knew the person well, my response was, "Respectfully, you aren't the audience we are trying to reach, and podcasts are quite popular with that audience." Thankfully, laughter ensued and a podcast was recorded. In a post-truth world, we don't have the luxury of allowing our personal biases to influence advertising spend.

DOES TRADITIONAL MEDIA STILL WORK?

This discussion about social media probably begs the question in every marketer's mind about whether there is still value in traditional media such as radio, billboards, TV, magazines, and newspapers.

The short answer is yes—they still have value for certain purposes and certain audiences. Traditional media plays an important but diminishing part in the mix. Of course, it's not like it was several decades ago, when we only had a few freely available channels, and everyone was watching Johnny Carson and saw the same TV ads, no matter what part of the country you lived in. Today, you can target much more than you used to.

It's not as if marketers are devoting the majority of their budget to prime time ads on ABC, NBC, or CBS. They are generally buying spots around local news (which is still heavily broadcast). They are buying spots on ESPN, Lifetime, and dozens of other niche channels that serve specific audience cohorts.

Those spots are mostly important when we are communicating something that we need all—or at least broad swaths—of our constituents to know and understand. There is still some value in the ability to tells lots of people the same thing simultaneously.

At the same time, the need to do that—to talk to everyone about the same thing in the same way—has dramatically shrunk.

This takes us back to our whole premise around the post-truth era. If we don't all accept the same facts at the center of our discussion, it is very difficult to say the same thing to multiple people and expect it to resonate in the same way.

Gone are the days when everyone could watch an unbiased (or perceived to be unbiased) personality like Walter Cronkite in the 1960s and come away with the feeling they had all watched and believed the same thing.

Depending on where you go and what you believe, you can find every element of your life to align around your viewpoint so you never have to be exposed to information you disagree with again.

It's true with media (especially social media), religion, friendships, politics, education, and every facet of life.

Will there continue to be a place for traditional media in marketing? Absolutely. But it will have to center around things that are less rooted in institutional or expert-driven opinion. It will need to be more personal and emotional in a way that cuts across multiple demographics.

In the next chapter, we will bring everything we have learned so far to bear on our final mile marker of authentic healthcare marketing: measurement.

CHAPTER SEVEN

MILE MARKER #5— MEASUREMENT

At this point in the marketing journey, it's time to think about how well your campaign has worked. It sounds counterintuitive, I know, but many marketers need to devote more time and resources to measuring the impact of their work—and the real, tangible business results.

It is easy to criticize people in the C-suite for always asking if their marketing dollars are working. But they have a valid point. Every marketer should be concerned about the ROI of not just their dollars, but also of their time and creative energy.

In this chapter, we will briefly explore the value of measuring your marketing efforts.

REAL-TIME OPTIMIZATION VS. STRATEGIC REVIEW

Once a campaign has been launched, we have the ability to optimize during flight. In real time, we can look at your dashboard, and even your authenticity scores (when we can survey for them), in order to optimize campaigns.

More importantly, real-time optimization is possible in performance marketing with Unlock's Media Control Platform, which allows us to optimize digital media buys in real time rather than adjusting SEM buys once every week or every month. Our proprietary algorithm enables the most efficient and cost-effective patient acquisition spend in the industry.

Every so often, a more purposeful review of effectiveness should take place. This should happen perhaps once every six months, or annually, depending on spend levels, company culture, marketing communications needs, or at the end of a campaign cycle.

We can take a whole range of inputs into account: engagement data, authenticity measures, brand perception shift measures, patient volumes, retention, acquisition, or whatever the effort was trying to achieve. This 360-degree review should determine how successful the effort has been overall and inform future efforts.

MEASURING A CHANNEL'S EFFECTIVENESS

Everyone in marketing will want to know the ROI on their use of particular channels. Not only because they want to do their jobs well, but because they will ultimately be accountable to the C-suite for how they allocate their budget. In a world of slim margins and constricted budgets, you must be able to communicate effectively with your CFO and CEO about ROI, or you will find *your* budget slimming as well.

It's important to know that you can't assess effectiveness the same way on every channel. For instance, your goals in a broadcast situation will be more about viewership, awareness, and preference—aspects that are more top of the funnel. You can use specific CTAs that make the impact more trackable and measurable. When you start dipping down into channels where impact and response is more measurable, other data come into play.

In digital media, one of the most important metrics is cost per acquisition (CPA) or sometimes similar measures such as Cost per Opportunity (CPO). How much money am I spending to educate and acquire a patient—meaning a patient needs to pick up the phone and make a call, or go to a website and schedule an appointment. How much does that cost compared with the eventual revenue that will come from treating that patient?

PR firms historically measured media impressions and reach. But today we are more focused on aspects like sharing your voice in a forum where you know there will be dialogue around certain topics.

How much of that is represented by us and our brand versus more quantitative measures in direct marketing, where you can measure the impact of each dollar in helping you acquire customers?

When someone asks how to know if a specific channel is effective, the short answer is that it depends on a variety of factors.

Real ROI measurement requires heavy lifting on the part of the marketing department and cooperation from finance. Most CRM systems produce estimates for ROI that CFOs quickly discount. However, true ROI is calculated by looking at the real revenue generated by patients acquired and retained by marketing, validated by the provider's own financial information or claims data, or both.

Of course, some negotiation is required to be sure the CFO agrees with the marketing department's definition of attribution, and this can vary by service line or site of care or patient cohort. Yet real ROI measurement aligns marketing's focus with the financial goals of the organization—nothing else can do that.

Once again, Rob Klein of Klein & Partners shares some wisdom that gets to the heart of the issue:

> Klein & Partners' 2024 National Consumer Insights Study revealed that the majority of consumers have used their mobile device to search for health information, compare providers, choose a provider, schedule a visit online, have a virtual visit, contact their provider with a question, refill a prescription, and pay a medical bill—and they probably didn't even leave the couch if they were sick! The digital highway is expanding at an accelerated rate for our "future" customers. If we don't jump on that highway with them and build credibility while they just need simple routine care, when it comes time for serious care, we may have already lost them. Again, authenticity is not just what you say but where you say it. Furthermore, the battle for market share is being fought at the top of the sales funnel for routine care today.[18]

---

18 Klein, unpublished white paper.

EXPERIENCES WITH DIGITAL HEALTHCARE
GEN Z / MILLENNIALS

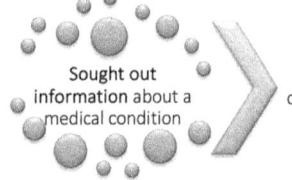

Sought out information about a medical condition

Compared what different providers offer before choosing where to go

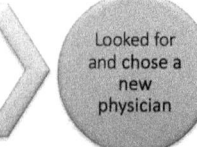

Looked for and chose a new physician

55% / 55%   **48% / 37%**   **40% / 33%**

(Re)filled a prescription

Paid a medical bill

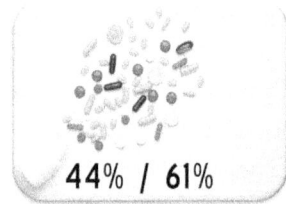

44% / 61%

52% / 56%

Scheduled a health care visit, test, procedure, etc.	**66% / 61%**
Had a virtual or telehealth visit with a provider	**39% / 41%**
Contacted your provider with a question or issue	**53% / 52%**

Share condition-related data with your provider using a smart watch or other wearable device

Manage your overall health using a digital tool that interacts with your provider

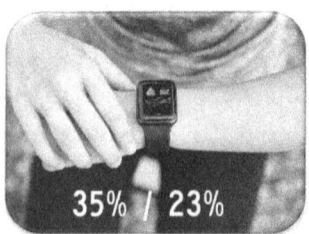

35% / 23%

51% / 41%

Source: Klein & Partners

That has been my goal in this chapter and this book as a whole: to get you on the highway where your ideal consumers are traveling.

If you can meet them there with a message that is authentic to your brand, it can open up a whole new world of possibilities.

CHAPTER EIGHT

WHAT DOES SUCCESS LOOK LIKE?

In the last five chapters, we have walked through five key mile markers on the journey to more authentic healthcare marketing. These are critical components for reaching your audience in a post-truth world and helping them receive the care they need.

In this chapter, we'll consider what it looks like when you're successful at implementing these keys. I want to paint a clear, compelling, and hope-filled picture of what you can achieve when you follow these principles.

After all, this isn't just marketing-speak or philosophical ideas. When it comes to healthcare, it can literally be a life-or-death issue.

THE MOST MEANINGFUL METRIC

At the highest level, the most important measurement of success is whether you are connecting people to the care they need so they can live better lives.

This contrasts with how many marketers define success: *Did I get you to think the right thing?*

That measurement of success involves a focus on brand awareness and brand preference. But what I'm talking about isn't just getting people to think or believe certain things. Authentic marketing means that we are connecting them to the right care at the right time—which means getting people to actually do something, not just think a certain way. Authentic marketing provides messages that are mission-driven, fact-based, and truthful. But it also engages *with* people, moving beyond the traditional approaches that talk *at* them.

If you back up from that overall goal of getting people the care they need, however, it does involve getting people to think certain things in terms of the credibility of the organization doing the marketing.

This is why you have to be a credible source of information to them. You also have to be an available source of real care. They should see you as a viable, authoritative, and caring entity that understands who they are and what they need.

If people don't have some level of trust in that, they certainly won't be inclined to seek you out for their care. They may also steer others away from you for the same reason.

ESTABLISHING CREDIBILITY

Following up on that baseline metric, other measurements are much more specific or quantitative. How well are you reaching cohorts you haven't reached before?

If we were having this conversation twenty or thirty years ago, we might ask some of these questions:

- How effectively am I reaching into the uninsured or Medicaid population?
- How well am I reaching people who are on public assistance?
- How well am I reaching immigrant populations, people who do not speak English as their primary language, and others who could be difficult to access?

Today, however, we would focus on these kinds of questions:

- How well am I reaching people from all corners of society in the post-truth era?
- How well am I reaching audiences who have varied levels of trust in traditional experts?
- How can I be a credible source or information to these groups and help them get the care they need … even if I don't agree with their beliefs?

Let's be honest: It's easy to write people off if we perceive that they believe something considered to be on the fringe. Yet our mission as healthcare providers is not just to provide care for people who are smart and pay attention. Our mission is to care for people in need. Did we decide we didn't want to engage because they wouldn't listen to us when we offered options for treatment? Are they wrong if they refuse treatment, or have they selected what they believe is right for them?

When we write them off, it's to their detriment and ours. We must reach out to all audiences with credibility, no matter what they believe, and regardless of the channels we have to go through to get to them.

A WORD TO THE C-SUITE

In writing this book, I have worked under the assumption that most of my readers will be people who are responsible for marketing in healthcare organizations, such as CMOs, marketing directors, or their staff members.

However, I also realize that others from the C-suite might be reading this as well. If you're a CEO, CFO, CSO, or are otherwise at the organizational level of leadership, I want to share a few thoughts about the value of the perspective I've shared in this book.

It's unfortunate that marketing in healthcare has accepted its status as a cost center instead of a value driver. We have accepted that CEOs and CFOs see it as a "nice to have" instead of a "must have."

I can't begin to tell you how many CFOs I have heard say, "We were going to get those patients anyway. I don't know how to credit marketing for that. It all comes from doctor and patient referrals."

The reason you should care about marketing is because of your mission. The ultimate measure of success for marketing is whether you have connected people to care. You can measure the impact of your work on bringing patients in and the impact it has on revenue when those people might have gone somewhere else, or perhaps nowhere at all.

In other words, the financial aspect—the ROI in marketing— is merely a measure of doing the right thing in the first place, which is getting people connected to care.

The way we know whether or not our marketing has worked is by measuring how many patients we brought in that we might not have gotten otherwise. How much revenue came with those patients?

That may sound a bit crass and capitalistic. Yet, after all, money is how we keep score in business. Even in the healthcare provider business.

If you follow the principles I've laid out in this book, you should soon be generating better ROI on your marketing spend because you will be meeting people where they are. As a result, you will authentically connect with audiences you haven't effectively reached before.

In any rational organization, if marketers can demonstrate the impact of an initiative on the bottom line, they will have much more credibility when it comes time to ask you for budget. You will look at marketing as a driver of revenue instead of a cost center.

THE RISK OF DOING NOTHING

Before we move on to the final chapter, where I will share next steps you can take on this journey, it's important to look at what could happen if you do nothing.

After all, doing nothing is always an option. I ask you to consider, however, what would it cost you to ignore everything you've read in this book about the enormous cultural change that's the hallmark of our post-truth era? What is the risk to you?

I don't really need to spell it out for you because you already know what is going to happen if you continue on the same path, assuming nothing has changed.

First, we know that trust in experts is declining, and that people are going to find healthcare marketing less credible and effective in the future if we don't change our approach.

And second, if your mission as a healthcare organization is to serve your community, there is a good chunk of people who are never going to hear your message. A subset of the population receives their information and makes decisions in different ways and from different channels than those you've been using to reach people.

If you don't change, there is a whole segment of people who won't be getting the care they need, and you will serve a smaller population than you were serving five or ten years ago.

Why? Because those people have tuned you out. You haven't earned the right to their attention. It's a harsh reality, but it doesn't make it any less true.

In the popular TV show *Mad Men*, set in the 1960s world of New York City advertising, marketing people were portrayed as creative and cool. I would love to see us return to that vibe, maybe minus the lunchtime drinking, constant smoking, and other cultural issues. But today, many marketers in healthcare are so tied to what has worked in the past that they aren't willing to change.

Where is the risk-taking? The innovation? The desire to rush headlong into the future and make something exciting happen?

We can't predict the future, but we can help create it. I've written this book to help people just like you create a better future, one where we aren't afraid to reach as many people as possible, even if they are radically different from us.

Nothing could be more important to your mission.

YOUR NEXT STEPS

Let's take a moment to review the ground we've covered:

In Chapter One, we explored the **post-truth era** that presents a unique challenge for healthcare marketers.

In Chapter Two, I offered a blueprint for understanding **why your marketing must be authentic** and what that means.

In Chapter Three, we talked through **Mile Marker #1: Authentic Insights** to understand why good and helpful data is the place to begin with effective healthcare marketing.

In Chapter Four, we learned about **Mile Marker #2: Plan Design** to help you design a plan that meets the moment you're in.

In Chapter Five, we dove into **Mile Marker #3: The Message and the Messenger** to discover what authority and credibility look like in a post-truth world.

In Chapter Six, we discussed **Mile Marker #4: Marketing Channels**, and I encouraged you to consider which channels will help you reach various demographics.

In Chapter Seven, we explored **Mile Marker #5: Measurement** to learn why it's not enough to go through the activities of marketing—they must be measured to determine if they are producing the right results.

In Chapter Eight, we brought everything together to present a **vision of what authentic healthcare marketing looks like** when it's successful.

Now I want to challenge you to take the next steps. While it's one thing to understand what you need to do, it's quite another to put that knowledge into practice.

I've put together a free resource detailing big-picture takeaways that will help you apply what you've learned in *Authentic Healthcare Marketing*. To access it, please visit go.unlockhealthnow.com/authentic-healthcare-marketing/.

CONNECT WITH UNLOCK HEALTH

If you have asked yourself those questions, and done so honestly, you might have concluded that you need more help in unlocking and empowering your healthcare marketing.

If you're interested, I invite you to visit our website, UnlockHealth.com, for more resources. You can find information on The Healthcare Authenticity Index we developed for our industry, as well as more on Authentic Healthcare Marketing.

I'll conclude this brief book with a statement I made in the Introduction. It summarizes what this book is all about:

HEALTHCARE MARKETING IS ALL ABOUT CONNECTING PEOPLE TO CARE SO THEY CAN LIVE BETTER LIVES.

If you are someone who is engaged in healthcare marketing every day, or someone who is in the C-suite but has a vested interest in successfully marketing your healthcare organization, then you have a big challenge ahead of you.

Twenty years ago, you could assume that people were getting their information from mostly the same places. That's not the case anymore. In a post-truth world, people receive their news and information from a much more dispersed (and biased) network of social media, influencers, left- or right-leaning cable networks, and more.

Though this presents a challenge to everyone engaged in marketing, it also gives us a unique opportunity to lean in and understand the views of patients and audiences who may see the world differently than we do.

You can dismiss some of their views as conspiracies, too reliant on the "wisdom of the crowds" at the expense of facts and science. Sometimes that is fair, and sometimes it's not. But if you don't understand how people think and what makes them tick, it's pretty hard to reach them, because you've already lost the game.

I hope this book will indeed help you connect people to the care they need so they can live better lives.

Onward and upward.

I've put together a free resource detailing big-picture takeaways that will help you apply what you've learned in *Authentic Healthcare Marketing*.

To access it, just scan this code:

WORKS CITED

Advertising Research Foundation. *"Cigna–'TV Doctors of America.'"* YouTube video, 0:48. June 28, 2017. https://youtu.be/0pYoyQCau5k.

Advisory Board. "See how American trust in healthcare is falling, in 5 charts." Advisory Board Daily Briefing, January 30, 2025. https://www.advisory.com/daily-briefing/2025/01/30/health-information-trust-poll.

Edelman. "2025 Edelman Trust Barometer." Edelman Trust Institute, January 2025. https://www.edelman.com/trust/2025/trust-barometer.

Godin, Seth. *All Marketers Are Liars*. New York: Portfolio, 2012.

Keyes, Ralph. *The Post-Truth Era: Dishonesty and Deception in Contemporary Life*. New York: St. Martin's Press, 2004.

KFF. "KFF Tracking Poll on Health Information and Trust: January 2025." Last modified January 28, 2025. https://www.kff.org/health-information-and-trust/poll-finding/kff-tracking-poll-on-health-information-and-trust-january-2025/.

Klein, Rob. Unpublished white paper. March 7, 2025. Provided to the author.

Lagasse, Jeff. "Class Action Lawsuit Against UnitedHealth's AI Claim Denials Advances." *Healthcare Finance News*, February 4, 2025. https://www.healthcarefinancenews.com/news/class-action-lawsuit-against-unitedhealths-ai-claim-denials-advances.

MacCracken, Linda. Document sent to the author. March 8, 2025.

RAND Corporation. "About Truth Decay." Last modified January 16, 2018. https://www.rand.org/research/projects/truth-decay/about-truth-decay.html.

Rucker, Patrick, Maya Miller, and David Armstrong. "How Cigna Saves Millions by Having Its Doctors Reject Claims Without Reading Them." *ProPublica*, March 25, 2023. https://www.propublica.org/article/cigna-pxdx-medical-health-insurance-rejection-claims.

Schleifer, Theodore, and Shane Goldmacher. "Future Forward, Backing Kamala Harris, Is Now the Biggest Spender in the 2024 Race." *The New York Times*, October 17, 2024. https://www.nytimes.com/2024/10/17/us/elections/future-forward-kamala-harris-ads.html.

Streaks, Jennifer. "Medical Bankruptcy: What It Is, What It Means, and Why It's So Common in the United States." *Business Insider*. September 16, 2024. https://www.businessinsider.com/personal-finance/credit-score/medical-bankruptcies.

Trelstad, Brian, Nien-hê Hsieh, Michael Norris, and Susan Pinckney. "Patagonia: 'Earth Is Now Our Only Shareholder.'" Harvard Business School Case 323-057, March 2023. Revised September 2023. https://www.hbs.edu/faculty/Pages/item.aspx?num=63834.

Weber, Larry. *Authentic Marketing: How to Capture Hearts and Minds Through the Power of Purpose*. Hoboken, NJ: Wiley, 2018.

WOULD YOU REVIEW THIS BOOK?

If you enjoyed reading *Authentic Healthcare Marketing*, would you kindly take a few moments to leave a review wherever you purchased it (and perhaps even on Goodreads.com)? We're grateful for your support. Thank you.

GRATITUDE

A book like this is the product of multiple minds coming together and contributing content. We owe gratitude to multiple people from Unlock Health who took time out to contribute: Christian Barnett, Ben Fuqua, Kevin Thilborger, Devon Barber, David Stump, Bradford Masoni, Allyson Gilmore, Shannon Curran, Allyzon Zahorcak, Dan Lavelle, Jasmine Griffin, Luke Bemis, and others. If I missed anyone, I truly apologize.

The book also benefited from great content supplied by friends of Unlock including Rob Klein, Suzanne Hendery, Tamara Jurgenson, Marcos Irigaray, Dan Miers, Dalal Haldeman, Linda MacCracken, and Amy Comeau.

We are very grateful for the continued support of our investors, Amulet Capital and Athyrium Capital. Big thanks to Gabe Luft, Hondo Sen, Will Cooper, Jason Kahn, Michael O'Brien, Trevor Perry, Tom Taylor, Katie Ingram, Jay Rose, and Ramsey Frank. Unlock Health would not exist without their commitment and support.

I'm also grateful for Honorée Corder and her expert team for help with planning, writing, editing, designing, and publishing this book. Thanks to Dino, M.J., Alyssa, Mike, and Kent.

On a personal level, I am so grateful for my wife of nearly three decades, Michele Edwards. She has been our family's rock during three decades of business travel, extended absences, long work weeks, and so many hosted company Christmas parties and events. They say the best marriages are those where both sides believe they got the better end of the deal—in this case, I know for sure I did.

WHO IS BRANDON EDWARDS?

Brandon Edwards is the Chief Executive Officer and founder of Unlock. A resident of Nashville, Tennessee (the healthcare capital of the United States), he has worked in the industry for three decades.

After starting his career working for a United States senator and a member of the House of Representatives, Brandon shifted his career to the agency side before joining Tenet Healthcare. There he handled crisis communications for the Western Division and eventually the entire company before shifting to Corporate Strategy & Ventures for his final two years with the organization.

After leaving Tenet, Brandon rejoined his previous agency as President and owner and served there for eight years building a healthcare practice with his friend Joanne Thornton. That firm's work for real estate and natural resources clients caused struggles in 2009, and Brandon bought the healthcare practice he had helped build to create ReviveHealth in 2009.

Brandon served as chief executive officer and founder at Revive for thirteen years, and the agency won "Agency of the Year" or "Best Agency to Work For" (or both) thirteen times in thirteen years, becoming the most awarded agency in the history of healthcare marketing. Revive was, at the time, the largest agency serving only healthcare providers in the U.S.

After selling ReviveHealth to Interpublic Group (IPG) in 2016 and completing the earnout process, Edwards became Executive Chairman of Revive for eighteen months before leaving the firm at the end of 2022. He founded Unlock Health in February 2022 with longtime friend and colleague Shannon Hooper.

Brandon is a graduate of the University of California, Santa Barbara, with a bachelor's degree in political science, and the University of California, Los Angeles, with a master's degree in business administration from the Anderson School. He is married with three grown children and the world's best French bulldog, Wilbur.

WHO IS
SHANNON MCINTYRE HOOPER?

Shannon Hooper is the President and cofounder of Unlock Health. A passionate advocate for tech-enabled transformation in healthcare marketing and consumer engagement, Shannon has spent her career at the intersection of strategy, innovation, and growth.

Her journey began at Burson-Marsteller (now Burson, a WPP company), where she led global health technology clients through complex challenges as part of the healthcare and crisis communications teams. Her early focus on digital transformation led her to Care Innovations, a joint venture between Intel Corporation and General Electric, where she spearheaded communications efforts. It was there that she met Brandon Edwards, then CEO and founder of Revive, and they formed a long-standing partnership and friendship.

Shannon joined Revive in its early days, helping shape what would become the most awarded agency in the history of healthcare marketing. Over her tenure, she built and led the

Health Technology Practice, served as Chief Growth Officer, and even took on interim CFO responsibilities, playing a critical role in the agency's expansion. Following Revive's acquisition by Interpublic Group (IPG) in 2016 and the successful completion of its earnout, she transitioned to a leadership role in digital health.

As Chief Strategy & Product Officer at BehaVR (now RealizedCare), Shannon oversaw product development, data analytics, machine learning, and consumer experience for a venture-backed digital therapeutics company, further cementing her expertise in the convergence of healthcare, technology, and behavioral science.

In February 2023, Shannon and Brandon cofounded Unlock Health, leveraging their shared vision and deep industry expertise to redefine how healthcare organizations engage with consumers, optimize marketing, and drive measurable business outcomes.

Shannon holds an MBA from Duke University's Fuqua School of Business, where she was recognized as a Fuqua Scholar, awarded to the top 10 percent of the graduating class. She lives in Nashville with her husband and their two spirited rescue pups.